and The Wall
the Arcade

"True translation is transparent: it does not obscure the original, does not stand in its light, but rather allows pure language, as if strengthened by its own medium, to shine even more fully on the original. This is made possible primarily by conveying the syntax word-for-word; and this demonstrates that the word, not the sentence, is translation's original element. For the sentence is the wall in front of the language of the original, and word-for-word rendering the arcade."

Walter Benjamin, "The Translator's Task"

and The Wall
the Arcade

Walter Benjamin's Metaphysics
of Translation and its Affiliates

SHIMON SANDBANK

sussex
ACADEMIC
PRESS
Brighton • Chicago • Toronto

2 4 6 8 10 9 7 5 3 1

First published 2019 in Great Britain by
SUSSEX ACADEMIC PRESS
PO Box 139
Eastbourne BN24 9BP

Distributed in North America by
SUSSEX ACADEMIC PRESS
Independent Publishers Group
814 N. Franklin Street
Chicago, IL 60610

British Library Cataloguing in Publication Data
A CIP catalogue record for this book is available from the British Library.

Library of Congress Cataloging-in-Publication Data
Applied for.

ISBN 978-1-84519-995-1

Typeset and designed by Sussex Academic Press, Brighton & Eastbourne.
Printed by TJ International, Padstow, Cornwall.

Contents

Preface   vii

Introduction   1

CHAPTER ONE
The Metaphysics of Translation: (1) No Reader   5

CHAPTER TWO
The Metaphysics of Translation: (2) Inessential Meaning   11

CHAPTER THREE
The Metaphysics of Translation: (3) Completion,   15
not Equivalence

CHAPTER FOUR
The Metaphysics of Translation: (4) Breaking Through   23
the Barriers of Language

CHAPTER FIVE
The Metaphysics of Translation: (5) Poetry is That which   27
Gains in Translation

CHAPTER SIX
The Colloidal Suspension   31

CHAPTER SEVEN
Benjamin and Paul Celan's Way to Pure Language   35

CHAPTER EIGHT
Pure Language   41

CHAPTER NINE
Aura and Translation   49

❤

Contents

CHAPTER TEN
Rosenzweig and Translation: Back Into Life   55

CHAPTER ELEVEN
Derrida and the King's Untouchable Body   61

CHAPTER TWELVE
The Practical Dimension   71

Notes   83
References   85
Index   89

Preface

After a lifetime as translator of English and German poetry into my mother-tongue, Hebrew, I felt a need to switch for a while from practice to theory and plunge into the wide sea of translation studies. It was only retroactively that I realized I had landed precisely on Walter Benjamin of all theorists because he too wrote his eccentric essay, "The Translator's Task", in the wake of his practice, namely his Baudelaire translations. The disparity, moreover, between his theory and his Baudelaire connected in my mind with my own strange preoccupation with a theory, Benjamin's, which has very little relevance to my own practice of poetry translation. For as translator of poetry I tend to think of myself as a poet manqué, unable to write my own poems but determined to rewrite others' poems in a way that would make them acceptable to the Hebrew reader. Benjamin, on the contrary, firmly rejects acceptability, aiming at breaking through the "rotten barriers" of his mother-tongue for the sake of maximum "kinship" with other languages and thereby advancing towards "Pure Language".

In spite of all this I found myself deeply interested in Benjamin's dissenting approach – perhaps *because* it is dissenting, and as such, opens up unexpected ways of looking at the craft of translation. In addition, I would like to acknowledge my debt to several sources that inspired my work. My colleague and friend, the late Stéphane Mosès, in his extraordinarily lucid writings,opened to me the gates to Benjamin's thought. The great poet Paul Celan, three volumes of whose poetry I translated, gave me some insight into the complicated alliance between the Jewish tradition and European modernism, in which the young Benjamin participated. The annual study-day initiated by Professor Vivian Liska in the Department of German Studies, The Hebrew University, gave me much food for thought in the field of Jewish German philosophy.

My thanks go also to Professor Moshe Ron who referred me to Derrida's "Monolingualism", to Professor David Fishelov for his encouragement, and to my university, The Hebrew University of Jerusalem, for their assistance.

DECEMBER 2018

For Tirza

Introduction

A random selection I once made of definitions of translation showed many differences in approach but a basic agreement. The early 19th century German philosopher Friedrich Schleiermacher and the popular present-day medium Wikipedia did not basically differ from each other. Schleiermacher did not use technical language and had the reader and his enjoyment in mind: "[...] the translator must take it as his goal to furnish his reader with just such an image and just such enjoyment as reading the work in the original language would have provided the well educated man" (Schleiermacher, p. 51). Wikipedia, on the other hand, used academic jargon and referred to text, not reader: translation is "the communication of the meaning of a source-language text by means of an equivalent target-language text". Both, however, shared three basic elements: (1) communication, (2) meaning, and (3) equivalence. Both took it for granted that translation had to do with **communicating** a foreign language message to a reader in his own language, and that the **meaning** of the translated message was meant to be the **equivalent** of the original one. Where Wikipedia has "communication" Schleiermacher has "furnishing one's reader"; "meaning" he calls "image", and "equivalent" – "just such". Both, however, see translation as the communication of equivalent meaning from one language to another.

Another element I found most discussions of translation included was the rule that "the structures of the source language will be preserved as closely as possible but not so closely that the target language structures will be seriously distorted" (Bassnett-McGuire, p. 2). The demand that the structures of the target language, with all fidelity to the source language, be left intact, recur in most descriptions of translations I came across. So, though less frequently, does the conviction that the translated text is inferior to the original. Voltaire has been sometimes quoted, "Translations increase the faults of a work and spoil its beauties", as has Robert Frost's famous maxim, "Poetry is what gets lost in translation".

In sum, the five elements I find recurring in most descriptions and definitions of translation are (1) translation as communication (2) translation as transferring meaning (3) translated meaning as equivalent of original meaning (4) translation preserving the structures of the target language (5) translation as inferior to its original.

I must add that, unlike points (1), (2), and (3) which seem universal, (4) and (5) are not so. The structures of the target language are not always considered sacred. The history of translation shows many variations on the relationship between original and translation, or writer and reader. Different periods see it differently, some "leaving the writer in peace as much as possible"' as Schleiermacher puts it, and "moving the reader toward him", while others "leave the reader in peace as much as possible and move the writer toward him" (Schleiermacher, p. 49). That is, some respect the original to the degree that they are willing to" seriously distort" their own language in the hope to convey the original as adequately as possible, while others respect the reader's habits of reading and regard his natural and pleasurable acceptance of the translated text as more important than maximum fidelity to the original text. As for point (5), the views regarding the relative quality of original and translation (the inferiority of the latter, its commensurability with the original, or even its superiority to it) likewise fluctuate, depending, like the relationship between source language and target language, on cultural and even political factors.

The importance and authority of Walter Benjamin's 1923 essay "Die Aufgabe des Übersetzers" or "The Translator's Task" (Benjamin 2012) lie in the way he revolutionized, not only points (4) and (5), but, more surprisingly, (1), (2), and (3) as well. Revolutionized, as far as the first three points are concerned, is an understatement: he minimized their role and may even be said to have done away with them. Translation, to Benjamin, excludes communication and equivalence, and reduces meaning to a minimum. Translation, to him, ignores communication with the reader, has to do with something other than meaning, and is not judged by similarity to the original.[1] In addition, it deliberately aims at overthrowing the structures of the target language (point 4) and its products are supposed to be superior to the original (point 5).

Discussing the pros and cons of this bold re-thinking of the nature of translation will be my task in the following chapters. After a general discussion of the five points I just mentioned (Chapters One to Five), I shall consider the mysterious way in which original becomes translation in the translator's mind (Ch. Six), Paul Celan's version of this mysterious way (Ch. Seven), the concept of "Pure" or "True" Language (Ch. Eight), Benjamin's late essay "The Work of Art in the Age of Mechanical Reproduction" and its relevance to his theory of translation (Ch. Nine), Franz Rosenzweig's theory of translation versus Benjamin's (Ch. Ten), Jacques Derrida's affinity with – and deviation from – Benjamin (Ch. Eleven), and finally some conclusions concerning the relevance of all this to the concrete practice of translation (Ch. Twelve).

Benjamin's essay was written as an introduction to his own translation of Baudelaire's *Tableaux Parisiens*, but has little to do with it. Perhaps he is "a great translation *thinker* who is not a great translator" (Berman, p. 38). Or otherwise, his discussion of translation is abstract to a degree that can be said to make it quite irrelevant to the practical demands of translation, including his own. And yet, its implications for the concrete process of poetry translation are substantial enough to deserve the further thinking attempted in our last chapter.[2]

Chapter One

The Metaphysics of Translation
(1) No Reader

When seeking insight into a work of art or an art form, it never proves useful to take the audience into account. [...] every effort to relate art to a specific public or its representatives [is] misleading [...] no work of art presupposes [man's] attentiveness. No poem is meant for the reader, no picture for the beholder, no symphony for the audience [...] If translation were intended for the reader, then the original would also have to be intended for the reader. If the original is not created for the reader's sake, then how can this relationship allow us to understand translation? (Benjamin 2012, p. 75)

What first strikes one in Benjamin's essay "The Translator's Task" as strange if not perverse, is his claim that translation is not intended for the reader. The assertion that "no poem is meant for the reader, no picture for the beholder, no symphony for the audience" is puzzling enough, doing away as it does with what one supposes to be an obvious component of the literary/artistic/musical act; but to apply the same to translation and claim that it, too, is not meant for the reader seems utterly absurd. Isn't the reader who does not know the language of the original the very *raison d'être* of translation? And is the argument from the (controversial) irrelevance of the reader to the poem to his irrelevance to translation valid? Even if a poem is not created "for the reader's sake", does this apply to its translation as well?

The answer lies in an earlier essay by Benjamin, "On Language as Such and on the Language of Man" (Benjamin 1979, pp. 107–123). The two youthful texts, "On Language as Such" of 1916 and "The Translator's Task" of 1921 (appeared in 1923), propose what Stéphane Mosès, in his book *The Angel of History*, defines as a "theological paradigm of history" (Mosès 2009, p. 68). They complement one another perfectly, says Mosès, so that both draw a perfect schema of human history, from its origins to its final fulfillment. At the same time, they are radically opposed by the tendency that animates them: 'On Language as Such and on the language of Man' presents human history as a process of decline, while 'The Translator's Task' describes it as a progress toward a utopian fulfillment. But those two contrary movements come together to trace the curve of original sin, and Fall, followed by a process of purification and progress toward renewal. Decline and restoration, degradation and Redemption, those two phases of sacred History define the theological vision of history in Benjamin. (Mosès 2009, pp. 69–70)

To Benjamin, this "theological vision of history" is a history of language. Under the influence of Kabbalistic language mysticism, to which he was introduced by his friend Gershom Scholem, the linguistic essence of reality – the infinite combinations of the letters of the Hebrew alphabet as underlying each and every sphere of existence – became central to his metaphysics.[3] "The indissoluble link between the idea of the revealed truth and the notion of language", writes Scholem many years later in "The Name of God and the Linguistic Theory of the Kabbala", "[...] is presumably one of the most important, if not the most important, legacies bequeathed by Judaism to the history of religions" (Scholem 1972, p. 60). Scholem showed, to quote Mosès, that "the mystical conception of language, that is, above all the idea that the essence of the real is linguistic and that that linguistic essence is a revelation of the Absolute, is a fundamental element of the Jewish tradition" (Mosès 2009, p. 170). The young Benjamin, in Scholem's wake, adopted this mystical conception of language in the two essays under discussion.

To go back to the question of the elimination of the reader from the act of translation, it must be understood as an upshot of this mystical philosophy of language. Once the essence of the real is said to be linguistic, any linguistic phenomenon, including translation, becomes part of metaphysics, the exploration of reality. As such, it calls for a radically new approach. Translation loses its instrumental role as a means of communication addressed to a reader, and becomes a cosmic occurence in a theological paradigm of history.

The concept of language presented in "On Language as Such and on the Language of Man", says Benjamin, is diametrically opposed to the "bourgeois" one, which claims that "the word has an accidental relation to its object, [...] it is a sign for things [...] agreed by some convention"

(1979, p. 117). The author of this concept of language is not mentioned, but Benjamin is clearly referring to Ferdinand de Saussure's theory of the arbitrariness of the linguistic sign. If the "bourgeois" view "holds that the means of communication is the word, its object factual, its addressee a human being", Benjamin's own, in contrast, "knows no means, no object, and no addressee of communication" (p. 111). Instead of being an instrumental "means of communication" with an object and an addressee, language, in its original, deep, meaning, is an object-less and addressee-less expression of inner life, which embraces the whole of creation: " There is no event or thing in either animate or inanimate nature that does not in some way partake of language, for it is in the nature of all to communicate their mental meanings" (p. 107). According to this mystical linguistics, not only nature but inanimate things too have a language to express themselves, a language given to them in creation and from which, "soundlessly ", "the word of God shines forth" (p. 117). The concept of language as identical with the divine Fiat, and things as God's words, could not be further away from de Saussure's accidental and arbitrary relationship between signifier and signified, word and thing.

The language of things, however, is "nameless"; "God made things knowable in their names", but it is man that "names them according to knowledge" (p. 115).[4] Man, in other words, "is the knower in the same language in which God is creator" (p. 116). It is at this point that the concept of translation is introduced – as "the translation of the language of things into that of man" (p. 117), or the nameless into name, or the knowable into the known. Translation is thereby lent a status "at the deepest level of linguistic theory"; "it is much too far-reaching and powerful to be treated in any way as an afterthought, as has happened occasionally." (ibid.) It no longer means what it has meant all along its history – the communication, as equivalent as possible, of a linguistic object from addressor to addressee. It is upgraded to a metaphysical level and spells a cosmic transition from the "mute to the sonic" (ibid.) and from the nameless to name. And since this transition is only a first phase in a "continuum of transformations"[5] – followed by the Fall and the Tower of Babel, and the subsequent differentiation of the original perfect knowledge into a multiplicity of languages (p. 119) – translation can be said to govern linguistic history, that is human history as such.

The first transformation, from nameless into name, or from inanimate to human, is obviously a huge advance – it is "the translation of an imperfect language into a more perfect one" (p. 117). The Fall, however, and the Tower of Babel that followed it, led to a tragic transformation from name language to the "human word", the "stepping outside the purer language of name", and making language a "means", a " mere sign" (p. 120). "In the Fall, man abandoned immediacy in the communication of the concrete, name, and fell into the abyss of the mediateness of all communication, of the word as means, of the empty word, into the abyss of prattle" (ibid.). It is this loss of immediacy and fall into "mediateness" that results in the plurality of languages, for once man turns away from the contemplation of things, and the immediate connection between name and thing is replaced by an arbitrary coupling of signifier and signified, man is deprived of the common foundation of his Adamic language, and "linguistic confusion" leads to its breakdown into multiple languages.

Benjamin thus distinguishes three stages in his mystical history of language. This is how Stéphane Mosès defines them:

> The first, in which the divine word appears as creator (Genesis 1:1–31), indicates language in its original essence, where it coincides perfectly with the reality it designates. At that primordial level, to which man never has had and never will have access, the duality of the word and the thing does not yet exist; in it, language, in its very essence, is the creator of reality.

> The second stage is that in which [...] Adam names the animals. This act of naming establishes the original language of man, lost today, but whose echoes are still heard for us through the symbolic, that is, poetic, function of language. [...] language and reality are no longer identical, but there is a sort of pre-established harmony between them [...]

> In the third stage, this 'paradisiacal language' [...] has been lost and degraded into a simple instrument of communication [...] From the abso-lute precision of naming, language falls into the 'abyss of prattle'. (Mosès 2009, p. 71)

If the bulk of "On Language as Such and on the Language of Man" laments the deterioration of language, its conclusion surprises with an "antithesis that permeates the whole sphere of language" (p. 123). Since, beyond communicating the communicable, language, even in its deteriorated state, is also "a symbol of the uncommunicable" and reflects a "residue of the creative Word of God", it can be restored, in a utopian future, to its pure origin in God: "All higher language is a *translation* of those lower, until in ultimate clarity the word of God unfolds, which is the unity of this movement made up of language [die Einheit dieser Sprachbewegung]" (p. 123, my italics).

It is not by chance that the word "translation" (Übersetzung) recurs in this final sentence. The emanation of language from God to the lowest forms and its utopian return to God are all conceived by Benjamin in terms of translation. Translation à la Benjamin, thus, has nothing to do with our "bourgeois" concept of it. Rather than the transition from one individual language to another for the sake of those who do not know the former, translation becomes the transformation of language "as such" from one plane of existence to another, from God to nature and man, and through man back to God.

The task of the translator, thus, goes far beyond his traditional task of linguistic interpretation for the sake of a specific public. His task is to contribute his share, small as it may be, to a cosmic process of returning language to its pure state, not in the initial, divine stage of linguistic history, which remains ever inaccessible, but in the ensuing human stage, in man's Adamic existence. Translation takes place, not between translator and reader, but between two texts, lower and higher, imperfect and more perfect, less immediate and more immediate, further from God and nearer to him. The translator carries out this task, toiling in God's service to liberate both word and thing from the long night of separation from Paradise.

Chapter Two

The Metaphysics of Translation
(2) Inessential Meaning

Fidelity and freedom – the freedom of rendering in accord with the sense and in its service, fidelity to the word – these are the old, traditional concepts in every discussion of translation. They no longer seem useful for a theory that seeks in translation something other than the reproduction of meaning [...] the translation's language can, indeed must, free itself from bondage to the sense, in order to allow its own mode of *intentio* to resound, not as the *intentio* to reproduce, but rather as harmony, as a complement to the language in which it is communicated. (Benjamin 2012, pp. 80–81)[6]

Benjamin's promotion of translation to a metaphysical status entails, as we have seen, the elimination of the reader from the translation process. In Benjamin's terms this is logical enough, as the reader's needs are irrelevant to a cosmic enterprise aiming at "the great motive of integrating the plurality of languages into a single true language" (2012, p. 80). Less obvious is the connection between Benjamin's theory and the marginalization of another basic factor of the literary act: meaning, or sense. But that is what he seems to be doing when he says that his theory "seeks in translation *something other* than the reproduction of meaning" (ibid., my italics).

On the face of it, the reproduction of meaning seems relevant, not only to the ordinary idea of translation, but to its Benjaminian metaphysical version as well. For the transition from the divine Fiat to the language of things, to human language, and back to the divine, must, though changing the mode of meaning, keep meaning itself as its object. At this point, however, a crucial factor comes in: unlike the earlier "On Language as Such", "The Translator's Task" explicitly deals from the outset not with language in general, but with the language *of poetry*: "What does *a poetic work* 'say', then? What does it communicate? Very little, to a person who understands it. Neither message nor information is essential to it" (ibid. p. 75, my italics) – i.e. essential to *a poetic work* (eine Dichtung), not to any text. The marginalization of message or meaning cannot apply to the translation of a purely informative text; it applies to literary translation only. To claim that the translation of a news item, for instance, must "seek something other than the reproduction of meaning" would be absurd. For a translated poem, on the other hand, to be more than the reproduction of meaning, would be uncontested. Sir John Denham in the 17th century already took this for granted:

> for it is not his [the translator of poetry's] business alone to translate Language into Language, but Poesie into Poesie; and Poesie is of so subtle a spirit, that in pouring out of one Language into another, it will all evaporate; and if a new spirit be not added in the transfusion, there will remain nothing but a Caput mortuum. (Bassnett-McGuire, p. 59)

And to Benjamin, what "is there in a poetic work – and even bad translators concede this to be essential – besides a message? Isn't it generally acknowledged to be the incomprehensible, the secret, the 'poetic'?" (2012, p. 75). It is the "poetic" beyond the message that poetry translation must reproduce; the message is "inessential", and a bad translation can be defined as "inexact transmission of inessential content" (ibid.).

The "inessentialness" of meaning in Benjamin's theory of translation can be traced back, it seems, to two influences: one poetic, French Symbolisme, and the other metaphysical, Jewish Kabbala.

The former often takes on a metaphysical stance which seems to verge on the latter. Benjamin's metaphysical concept of translation, the "great motive of integrating the plurality of languages into a single true language", cannot but remind one of Mallarmé's Symboliste dream of overcoming the diversity of languages and reaching the one language of truth: "the diversity on earth of idioms stops anyone from uttering the words which, otherwise, would find themselves to be, at a stroke, in substance truth itself" (Mallarmé 1977, p. 43). The words which could be "in substance truth itself", that supreme language, are to Mallarmé the "essential" condition of language, the one opposed to the "blunt or immediate" one, which refers to the reality of things and serves for communication. Essential – as distinct from immediate – speech distances things and makes them vanish (ibid., p. 45). The way natural things disappear in "essential" speech and are replaced by their essence is described in Mallarmé's famous lines:

> Why should we perform the miracle by which a natural object is almost made to disappear beneath the magic waving wand of the written word, if not to divorce that object from the direst and the palpable, and so conjure up its essence in all purity?

> When I say: 'a flower!' then from that forgetfulness to which my voice consigns all floral form, something different from the usual calyces arises, something all music, essence, and softness: the flower which is absent from all bouquets. (Mallarmé 1965, p. 112)

"Essential" speech, which makes palpable things vanish behind their musical essence, seems close to Benjamin's language of poetry, to which "neither message nor information is essential". This, not the other 'blunt' (or communicative) sort of language, is the language whose mode of 'intentio', way of meaning rather than meaning itself, he wants translation to give voice to. In Husserl's phenomenological terms, translation should give voice to the intentional *quality*, not the intentional *matter*, of the original (Husserl, pp. 119–122). Benjamin's above-quoted words, "The translation's language can, indeed must, free itself from bondage to the sense, in order to allow its own mode of intention to resound", are reminiscent of Mallarmé's letter to Cazalis of 30 October 1864: "Le vers ne doit donc pas, là, se composer de mots, mais d'intentions, et toutes les paroles s'effacer devant la sensation" ("the poetic line should not be composed of words but of intentions, and all words are effaced by sensation" (Mallarmé 1998, p. 663). Mallarmé's "intentions", as well as Benjamin's "mode of intention" or "Art des Meinens" (way of meaning[7]), refer to what transcends words themselves, or message, or referent. The "way of meaning" of the object "bread", to use Benjamin's example, is different in the French "pain" from the German "Brot", in spite of the fact that the referent is the same (2012, p. 78). It is the difference between the two *ways* of meaning, not the meant object itself, that the translator must bring to light. Mallarmé describes it as "something all music, essence, and softness", Benjamin – as "the incomprehensible, the secret, the 'poetic'". The translator's task is to recreate the "poetic" in the poem rather than reproduce its message.

Benjamin's way of meaning, however, what is "incomprehensible, secret and poetic" in it, is given a metaphysical ground. It is mystical in origin, for it largely derives from Jewish Kabbala and its mystical paradigm of the history of language.

When Adamic language deteriorates into our present, fallen type of language, losing the original unity of word and thing, it remains, beyond communicating the communicable, also a symbol of the uncommunicable, reflecting a "residue of the creative Word of God". Gershom Scholem regards this as "the point of departure of all mystical linguistic theories", a point –

> constituted by the conviction that the language – the medium – in which the spiritual life of man is accomplished, or consummated, includes an inner property, an aspect which does not altogether merge or disappear in the relationships of communication between men. Man passes on information, man tries to render himself comprehensible to other men, but in all such attempts there is something else vibrating, which is not merely communication, meaning and expression [...] what exactly is this 'secret' or 'hidden' dimension of language [...] it is the symbolic nature of language which defines this dimension [...] language is used to communicate something which goes way beyond the sphere which allows for expression and formation [...] a certain inexpressible something which only manifests itself in symbols, resonates in every manner of expression [...] something pertaining to [the] structure [of language] which is not adjusted to a communication of what is communicable, but rather [...] to a communication of what is non-communicable, of that which exists within it for which there is no expression; and even if it could be expressed, it would in no way have any meaning, or any communicable sense. (Scholem 1972, pp. 60–61)

It is this Kabbalistic "inexpressible something", beyond mere communication, that seems to at least partly underlie Benjamin's metaphysics of translation. The translator's task is to capture, not the comprehensible and communicative in the deteriorated language of post-lapsarian man, but its hidden, non-communicable, dimension. It is this dimension, the residue, or far echo, of Adamic language and indirectly of the word of God itself, that may lead man back, via translation, to his origin in God's Fiat. Mallarmé's "flower which is absent from all bouquets" seems to join the Kabbalistic inexpressible residue of God's word in Benjamin's concept of that which the translator's task is to translate.

Chapter Three

The Metaphysics of Translation
(3) Completion, not Equivalence

Once message or meaning is shown to be inessential to Benjamin's concept of translation, equivalence in meaning is no longer relevant. Benjamin's cosmic process of translation leaves little room for considerations of similarity or dissimilarity between original and translation. If translation is dynamic development, not static transmission of message, it does not strive to equal the original, but to go beyond, and complement, it.

The concept of translation as a dynamic progress from one language to another is not really new. Indeed, it goes back to the very beginnings of translation – to the age of the Romans and their cultural imperialism. The goal then, as the German theorist Hugo Friedrich puts it, was "to surpass the original"; "translation meant to conquer", in Nietzsche's words (Friedrich, p. 14). It was only in the eighteenth century that translators "began to see other languages as equals and not as inferior forms of expression in comparison to their own languages" (Schulte & Biguenet, p. 3). Thus, the notion of equivalent translation belongs to modern times.

To the Romans, and later to the Renaissance, the inferiority of foreign languages did not preclude their exploitation for one's own use: the goal was to surpass the original "and, in doing so, to consider the original as a source of inspiration for the creation of new expressions in one's own language", to release "those linguistic and aesthetic energies that heretofore had existed only as pure possibility in one's own language" (Friedrich, p. 13). Translation, thus, was considered from the outset as a dynamic process of perfection rather than a neutral transmission of subject matter from one verbal system to another.

Friedrich Schleiermacher, in his treatise "On the Different Methods of

Translation" (1813), makes the distinction we quoted earlier: "Either the translator leaves the writer in peace as much as possible and moves the reader toward him, or he leaves the reader in peace as much as possible and moves the writer toward him". Although Schleiermacher believes the two paths to be completely different from one another, "any attempt to combine them being certain to produce a highly unreliable result" (Schleiermacher, p. 49), the combination of the two seems to inform the idea of translation from its Roman start. For what does the use of the original as a source of inspiration for enriching one's own language mean? It means "moving the reader toward the writer" *only in order* to "move the writer toward the reader": acquainting the reader with a foreign set of mind in order to make an element of that set of mind enter into the reader's own language and become an integral part of it.

To go back to Benjamin, his metaphysical concept of translation as a cosmic progress toward – or back to – Adamic language, seems to assign a similar task to the translator: to go back to the language of the original in order to enrich his own language, to "broaden and deepen his own language through the foreign one", as the German writer Rudolf Pannwitz (1881–1969) puts it. Benjamin praises Pannwitz's views on translation and quotes him:

> our translations even the best start out from a false principle. They want to germanize Indic, Greek, English, instead of indicizing, graecizing, anglicizing German [...] the fundamental error of the translator is that he holds fast to the state in which his own language happens to be rather than allowing it to be put powerfully in movement by the foreign language. (2012, p. 82)

To be put in movement by the foreign language seems close to the ancient Roman position as formulated by Hugo Friedrich, "considering the original as a source of inspiration for the creation of new expressions in one's own language". It is, however, basically different: the Romans – and Pannwitz too – were above all aspiring to broaden their own language's field of reference, whereas Benjamin's project was to advance his language toward the Pure Language by introducing the original's ways of meaning and combining it with its own. For his ultimate goal was to reach to the single language of truth beyond all individual languages.

Once translation is seen as transformation and perfection, the relationship between original and translation must be other than equivalence. The concept of equivalence, as Benjamin says with regard to the concept of fidelity, "no longer seem[s] useful for a theory that seeks in translation something other than the reproduction of meaning" (p. 80). Instead, what it seeks is the manifestation in translation of the "kinship" of languages, a kinship "far deeper and more specific than [shown] in the superficial and indefinable similarity of two literary texts" (p. 77). This kinship goes back – and forward – to the one Adamic language, lost with the Fall and the Tower of Babel. If those cosmic catastrophes broke up the single "pure language of name" into the plurality of languages of "means" or mediateness, the translator's great task is to "[bring] the seeds of pure speech to maturation in translation" (p. 80); not to produce an equivalent copy of the original's meaning, but to make the original grow into "a linguistic sphere that is both higher and purer" (p. 79).

Benjamin's often-quoted simile for this concept of translation is that of a broken vessel:

> Just as fragments of a vessel, in order to be fitted together, must correspond to each other in the minutest details but need not resemble each other, so translation, instead of making itself resemble the sense of the original, must fashion in its own language, carefully and in detail, a counterpart to the original's mode of meaning, in order to make both of them recognizable as fragments of a vessel, as fragments of a greater language. (p. 81)

The juxtaposition of original and translation as two fragments of a broken vessel is rich in implications. Instead of resembling (gleichen) each other, they follow (folgen)[8] each other, and instead of surpassing – or falling short of – one another, they seem to be on equal standing. But in keeping with Benjamin's concept of translation as growth and perfection, the way the two "follow" each other is then defined as translation's fashioning (sich anbilden)[9] "a counterpart to the original's mode of meaning". And mode, or way, of meaning, as we have seen, is not the referent, but its connotations in a particular language; not the referent of the German "Brot", but the infinitely subtle and elusive difference between "Brot" and the French "pain" (p. 78). If that fragment of the vessel which stands for one of the translations is presented in Benjamin's simile as fitting the fragment which stands for the original, this is so because the translators have uncovered in the latter, and recreated in their own translation, a way of meaning that would "complement" the way of meaning of the target language. In Kabbalistic terms, the various fragments equally reflect God's creative word, which is the lost, non-communicable, entire, vessel.

One is struck by what seems like an amazing leap Benjamin is performing, with his image of the broken vessel, from mystical myth to the theory of translation. What in the lore of the great 16th century Kabbalist Isaac Luria is "a mystical interpretation of Exile and Redemption" (Scholem 1961, p. 286) becomes an image of the relationship between source language and its translations, and between both and the ultimate Pure Language. For the simile of the broken vessel is undoubtedly borrowed from Luria's doctrine of the "Breaking of the Vessels" and their "Tikkun", i.e. mending. The primeval lights emanating from God's attributes, the so-called "Sefiroth", were caught and preserved, according to this doctrine,[10] in vessels, but God's revealed light proved too much for the lower vessels and they were broken and shattered. As long as this damage is not mended, deficiency is inherent in everything that exists. The restitution, or "Tikkun", of the original whole is Messianic Redemption, the secret purpose of existence, achieved through the spiritual action of man.

The vessel as Pure Language, the "breaking of the vessels" as its deterioration and fallen state, the "Tikkun" as translation: all this seems rather fanciful, a jump from theology to linguistics. But if Benjamin's linguistic theory is religious, Kabbalah's religion can be said to be linguistic. Side by side with the light of the Sefiroth, language too, according to the Kabbalists, is the expression of God's hidden self; the symbolism of light and the symbolism of language, the sefiroth and the letters of the Hebrew alphabet, are two methods in which Revelation is represented in a symbolic manner. "The doctrine of emanation and the closely allied symbolism of light", to quote Scholem, "are intertwined with the mysticism of language and the symbolic interpretation of the letters as the hidden, secret signs of the divine in all spheres and stages which the process of the creation passes through" (1972 [part 2], p. 166). And, in the same way as creation is represented in terms of language, redemption, or the return to God from exile, is conceived in such terms as well. "Each and every word that was pronounced by God, was divided into seventy languages", says the Kabbalist Abraham Abulafia, and the scholar Moshe Idel adds: "Therefore, the divine word can be restored to its primordial perfection by returning the seventy languages to one original entity" (Idel, p. 173).

If language is a symbolic presentation of divine revelation, Benjamin's application of the "breaking of the vessels" and the "tikkun" to his theory of translation is less fanciful than would seem. The "breaking of the vessels" easily lends itself to the narrative, in "On Language as such and the Language of Man", of the deterioration of language, and "Tikkun" – to the return of language through translation to its original purity, described in "The Translator's Task". Abulafia's mystical ladder, "The Path of the Names", which begins with the combination of the letters of the Hebrew alphabet and ends with God's name (Scholem 1961, pp. 119–155), is recast in Benjamin's doctrine into a ladder of translations which begins with any text, including those in a foreign tongue, and gradually elevates it to the ultimate sphere. Each fragment of the shattered vessel is a version of the original text, perfected by the translator/mystic. "The mystic", as Scholem paraphrases Abulafia, "re-smelts all languages and recreates them in the one holy language" (1972 [part 1] p. 191). Replace "mystic" with "translator" and you get the essence of Benjamin's doctrine.

To go back to the question of equivalence, the "recreation" of the original by means of translation is not through an equivalent meaning, but, as we have seen, through the incorporation in it of a new mode or way of meaning, located in the source language and previously non-existent in the target language. The new mode of meaning is not a new meaning in the sense of a new "reference to some slice of reality" (Rabin, p. 123); it is rather the "incomprehensible" and "poetic," – the "essential" of the Symbolistes or the Kabbalist trace of the divine word – which is hidden in the original and transcends all meaning. The progress, via translation, toward the single Pure Language is by identifying the latter's "seeds" in the original and "bringing them to maturation" in the translation.

Rejecting equivalence, Benjamin describes the way translation relates to the original as harmony (Harmonie), complement or completion (Ergänzung): "[...] the translation's language can, indeed must, free itself from bondage to the sense, in order to allow its own mode of *intentio* to resound, not as the *intentio* to reproduce, but rather as harmony, as a complement to the language in which it is communicated" (p. 81). The translation's "intentio" meets that of the original and complements it as one more step (one more fragment of the vessel) toward the "pure language" (the entire vessel). This cannot be attained by any language alone, "but only by the totality of their mutually complementary intentions" (p. 78). "Pure language", to quote Berman, "is what each language wants to say (*meint*), but it can only be reached through the complementary totality of what all languages want to say" (Berman, p. 128).

To conclude this chapter, mention must be made of two brief essays written some ten years later, which focus on similarity in the relation between word and meaning: "Doctrine of the Similar" ("Lehre vom Ähnlichen") and its revised and abridged version, "On the Mimetic Faculty" ("Über das mimetische Vermögen"). What Benjamin calls "the mimetic faculty" is here claimed to be inherent to man both ontogenetically and phylogenetically: the child playing at being a windmill or a train, as well as the ancients reading the future or fate from stars or entrails. Both perceive a similarity which the modern grown-up can no longer perceive. The "perceptual world of modern man contains only minimal residues of the magical correspondences and analogies that were familiar to ancient peoples" (2005b, p. 721). But we too are able to perceive a "nonsensuous similarity" – and that is in *language*:

> . . . [the] mimetic gift, which was earlier the basis for clairvoyance, very gradually found its way into language and writing in the course of a development over thousands of years, thus creating for itself in language and writing the most perfect archive of nonsensuous similarity. In this way, language is the highest application of the mimetic faculty – a medium into which the earlier perceptual capacity for recognizing the similar had, without residue, entered to such an extent that language now represents the medium in which objects encounter and come into relation with one another. No longer directly, as they once did in the mind of the augur or priest, but in their essences, in their most transient and delicate substances, even in their aromas. (2005a, pp. 697–8)

Rejecting De Sassure's arbitrary system of signs, and believing that the "mimetic gift" is now manifest in language, Benjamin thus feels obliged to have recourse to the "onomatopoeic mode of explanation". He admits that the onomatopoeic explanation for the signifier–signified relationship is "primitive", but when "developed and adapted to improved understanding" it can shed light, he claims, on words as governed by a "nonsensuous similarity" between sound and meaning, and, indeed, between their written form (*Schriftbild*) and their meaning: "it is nonsensuous similarity that establishes the ties not only between what is said and what is meant but also between what is written and what is meant, and equally between the spoken and the written" (2005b, pp. 721–2).

Neither the first, nor the second, revised, essay provides an example of the "nonsensuous similarity" that governs language. The only example, in the first version, is of the relationship of the name of a letter to the name of the signified in which it participates: "[…] the letter *beth* {in Hebrew} is the root for the word meaning 'house'" (2005a, p. 696). The English version is misleading in this case, for the original German has: "So hat der Buchstabe Beth den Namen von einem Haus" (Benjamin 1991, p. 208), which literally means: "The letter beth has the name of house". What Benjamin seems to be saying is that the Hebrew letter "beth", included in "bayit" (Hebrew for "house"), bears a name the sound of which is identical with the sound of the Hebrew word in which it is included (particularly with the sound of its genitival form "beit"). Therefore, he seems to be saying, there is a "nonsensuous similarity" in this case between the signifier "beth" and the signified "bayit".

I think it is not by chance that this example is left out out in the revised version of the essay. For unlike the "similarity" between the child and the windmill, or between the stars and fate, the similarity between "beth" and "bayit" is not at all "nonsensuous". It is rather a case for the "onomatopoeic mode of explanation" which Benjamin brands as "primitive". The tie between "beth" and "bayit", indeed, is doubly "sensuous": both auditorilly (for their sound is similar) and visually (for the shape of the Hebrew letter "beth" is somewhat like a house). So that this can hardly be accepted as an example of language as a "perfect archive of nonsensuous similarity".

The above quotation concludes, however, with the words –

> language now represents the medium in which objects encounter and come into relation with one another. No longer directly, as they once did in the mind of the augur or priest, but in their essences, in their most transient and delicate substances, even in their aromas.

Ignoring Benjamin's questionable example, this description of "nonsensuous similarity" as an "encounter" between "objects" ("Dinge" in German) seems to concur with his earlier concept of the relationship we saw between original and translation. If the similarity he is now talking about is not "direct" but a relationship between objects – or words – "in their *essences*" or "most delicate substances", it perfectly agrees with the "mode of meaning", the *essential*, "incomprehensible" and "poetic", which the translator is expected to incorporate in his target language.

The "completion" that replaces "equivalence" in translation can thus be seen, from the perspective of the two essays under discusion, as a "nonsensuous similarity". Translation, like language itself, shows an encounter between objects "no longer directly" but "in their essences". The same "mimetic faculty" that governs the relation of "bread" to its signified in the real world, applies to the relation of "bread" to "Brot". It is the ladder that enables language to climb towards its "pure" state.

Chapter Four

The Metaphysics of Translation
(4) Breaking Through the Barriers of Language

"To be put powerfully in movement by the foreign language" – this is the above-quoted task of the translator according to Rudolf Pannwitz, approvingly quoted by Benjamin. But if Pannwitz, as we have seen, assigns him this task in order to "broaden and deepen his own language through the foreign one" (Benjamin 2012, p. 82), Benjamin uses Pannwitz's words to support his own theory. He wants the target language "to be put powerfully in movement" not for its own sake, but in order to serve as a step in the ladder leading to the ultimate language. The translator's task is "to set free in his own language the pure language spellbound in the foreign language, to liberate the language imprisoned in the work by rewriting it" – and "to this end he breaks through the rotten barriers of his own language" (ibid.).

Breaking through the "rotten", or decayed, barriers (*morsche Schranken*) of one's language contradicts the common translator's practice – to avoid seriously distorting the structures of his own language. But since the acceptability to the reader is irrelevant to Benjamin's metaphysical theory, the free remoulding, even distortion, of the target language is acceptable, indeed desirable, as long as it is conducive to the cosmic process that Benjamin envisages, to the "Fortleben", or continuing life (p. 79), of the original and its gradual purification.[11]

The reader of a translated text, thus, should be continuously reminded of its foreignness. Its foreignness, indeed, testifies to its value, whereas "it is not the highest form of praise to say [...] that [a translation] reads as if it were an original in its own language" (p. 81). Fidelity to the original shows in a *literal* translation, which expresses through its foreignness and its distortion of the structures of its language "the great longing for the completion of language" (ibid.). A translation which reads as if it were an original work makes the reader come to rest there instead of "completing" it.

How does a literal translation contribute to the "continuing life" of the original? How does it "set free" the pure language "spellbound" in the original, bringing "the seeds of pure speech to maturation?"

Benjamin answers:

> True translation is transparent: it does not obscure the original, does not stand in its light, but rather allows pure language, as if strengthened by its own medium, to shine even more fully on the original. This is made possible primarily by conveying the syntax word-for-word; and this demonstrates that the word, not the sentence, is translation's original element. For the sentence is the wall in front of the language of the original, and word-for-word rendering the arcade. (Ibid.)

The rather vague definition "conveying the syntax word-for-word" ("Wörtlichkeit in der Übertragung der Syntax"), when placed together with "the word, not the sentence [as] translation's original element" and "the sentence [as] the wall in front of the original", seems to mean that, rather than translating the meaning of the entire sentence, the translator's task, in order to break through the barriers of his own language, is to concentrate on the *single word* and its *syntactic relation* to the other words. This does not mean that the semantic content of individual words becomes irrelevant, but that –

> their significance is not determined through their intrinsic, conceptual content, but rather through the way in which the individual elements are syntactically related or positioned with respect to the other elements of the phrase. (Weber, pp. 76–77)

Or as Berman puts it:

> [...] there is no [...] contradiction in saying that the originary element of the translator is the word and, at the same time, that the translator's fundamental task is transposition, the transfer (*Übertragung*) of syntax. Because the word unfolds within the syntactical domain, not in the domain of the grammatical sentence. (Berman, p. 197)

The gist of Benjamin's theory, translation as playing down meaning and centering on the way of meaning, is that what counts is the word and its syntactic position, not the entire sentence. For sentence – or the German "Satz" – is statement, whereas word is the way in which you state; it is not only, to quote Paul de Man,"the agent of the statement as lexical unit, but also as syntax and as grammar" (de Man, p. 88). When Benjamin adds, "the word, not the sentence, is translation's original element [Urelement]", what he means, thus, is that word and syntax, rather than meaning, is what translation should convey. Meaning is the "wall" that blocks the light of the original, whereas word-for-word rendering is the "arcade" that lets it through. Thus, the "rotten barriers" of the translator's own language are its "ways of meaning", whose rigidity must yield to the incorporation of foreign ways of meaning.

The logical outcome is that "from the moment that a translation is really literal, wörtlich, word by word, the meaning completely disappears" (de Man, p. 29). Benjamin's radical example is Friedrich Hölderlin's trans-lations of Sophocles: they are, as de Man puts it, absolutely literal and therefore often unintelligible (ibid.). Or, in Benjamin's picturesque language, they are "inhabited by the monstrous and original danger of all translation: that the portals of a language broadened and made malleable in this way may slam shut and lock up the translator in silence" (2012, p. 83).

A quotation from Hölderlin's translation of Sophocles' *Antigone*, discussed by Antoine Berman, will serve to make this "monstrous" danger clear. Ismene's words to Antigone, "Τι δ εστι; ζηλοισ γαρ τι καλκαινουσ εποσ" ("What is it? 'Tis plain that thou art brooding on some dark tidings" in R.C. Jebb's translation) are literally rendered by Hölderlin as "Was ist's, du scheinst ein rotes Wort zu färben", i.e. "What's the matter, you seem to colour/dye a red word". In this example, Berman says, Greek and German "have indeed entered into perfect harmony, to the complete detriment of meaning". Furthermore, "at this one point the translation produces a *third* language that gestures towards the (absent) domain where languages are reconciled and complete each other" (Berman, p. 157).

I must admit I find it rather difficult to find either "perfect harmony" or a "third language" in Hölderlin's translation at this particular point. As we shall see later on, there are other lines in Hölderlin which support Benjamin's argument, but from a syntactic rather than semantic perspective. Another quotation which Berman borrows from George

Steiner, a Paul Celan translation of a poem by Supervieille which "[accentuates] its signifying density" (Berman, p. 158) can serve, I believe, as a better example of Benjamin's thinking, though less free from "meaning". I shall come back to it in Chapter 7.

Benjamin, however, is not unaware of the cul-de-sac which his theory must lead to: the silence of meaninglessness. But in the downright theological conclusion to his essay, as we shall see, he adds to language and meaning a third agent – Truth, the exclusive realm of Holy Scripture, where the mediation of meaning is no longer needed.

Chapter Five

The Metaphysics of Translation
(5) Poetry is That which Gains in Translation

Robert Frost's saying, "Poetry is that which gets lost in translation", is the most quoted – and most inimical – condemnation of translated poetry. Its popularity derives from the succinct way it expresses the common belief in the presumably incontestable superiority of original over translated poetry. This belief, however, was not always the norm.

For many centuries poetry, on the contrary, was that which gains much in translation. The main grounds for this view were nationalistic: the target language was regarded as belonging to a higher civilization than that of the source language, and its poetics were accordingly superior.

An imperialistic version of this approach lies, as we have seen, at the very beginning of the history of translation. The earliest, Roman, approach was not, however, free from ambivalence. The Greek civilization was both admired and looked down on. In Hugo Friedrich's words, "Latin cultural and linguistic imperialism [...] despises the foreign word as something alien but appropriates the foreign meaning in order to dominate it through the translator's own language" (Friedrich, p. 13) It is Latin "that dictates the rules", and it dictates them rather militantly, to judge from Saint Jerome's words in his treatise about translation: "The translator considers thought content a prisoner which he transplants into his own language with the prerogative of a conqueror" (pp. 12–13).

Many centuries later, the same nationalistic approach flagrantly informs the "Preface to the Reader" of Philemon Holland's *Historie of the World* (London, 1601), an English translation of Pliny the Elder's (Gaius Plinius Secundus') *Naturalis Historia*. In his Preface, Holland attacks those critics who claim that "these and such like books ought not to be published in the vulgar tongue", i.e. English, and that

"Latinists onely are to bee acquainted with [such books]". Such critics, he says, "think not so honourably of their native countrey and mother tongue as they ought", for if they did they would "wish rather and endeavour by all means to triumph now over the Romans in subduing their literature under the dent of the English pen, in requital of the conquest sometime over this Island, atchieved by the edge of their sword" (1601, no page number). Holland thus celebrates his own translation as a triumph over the Romans in revenge for their conquest of Britain in the distant past.

An equally comic celebration of translation in terms of national vendetta is that of the Hebrew novelist Peretz Smolenskin (1842–1885) in his introduction to Yitzhak Edward Salkinsohn's Hebrew translation of Shakespeare's *Othello* (1874). Smolenskin's Jewish nationalist convictions make him hold the translator's Hebrew to be a holy 'treasure house' which elevates the original English to its own glorious heights:

> 'Today we take revenge on the British! They took our Holy Scriptures and made them their own, translated them and spread them all over the world as if they were theirs. And we too repay them today for what they did: we have taken the book, that is as dear to them as our Holy Scripture is to us, and introduced it into the treasure house of our Holy tongue. Is not this revenge sweet?' (Almagor, Introductory Notes)

A subtler version of this nationalistic approach can be seen in those 18th century translators and theorists of translation that based the presumable superiority of their translations on poetic grounds. A French translator of the *Iliad*, Antoine Houdar De la Motte, finds his abbreviated version of Homer (1714) aesthetically superior to the original. In his introduction he writes:

> I have reduced the twenty four books of the *Iliad* to twelve, which are even shorter than Homer's. At first sight you might think that this could only be done at the expense of many important features. But if you pause to reflect that repetitions make up more than one sixth of the *Iliad*, and that the anatomical details of wounds and the long speeches of the fighters make up a lot more, you will be right in thinking that it has been easy for me to shorten the poem without losing any important features of the plot. I flatter myself with the thought that I have done just that, and I even think I have brought together the essential parts of the action in such a way that they are shaped into a whole better proportioned

and more sensible in my abbreviated version than in the original. (Bassnett & Lefevere, p. 22)

Later in that century, however, a development takes place towards an "increasing tolerance of cultural differences" and a "respect for the foreign", which leads to "the courage to move toward the foreign" (Friedrich, pp. 14–15). Of the above-quoted two paths open, according to Schleiermacher, to the translator, he now "leaves the writer in peace as much as possible and moves the reader toward the writer". In other words, adequacy to the source text is gradually being elevated over acceptability in the translating culture. No longer Pope's elegant Homer which had pleased the earlier generation's ear by transforming the Greek into the familiar and beloved pentameter couplets. Now the classical scholar Richard Bentley (1662–1742) can respond to Pope's *Iliad* with the words "It is a pretty poem, Mr. Pope, but you must not call it Homer" (Samuel Johnson 1967, p. 213, note2). To be called Homer, a translation must be literally faithful to the original, even at the risk of alienating its readers. The original is definitely superior to its translation; the latter can only hope to move us nearer to the former.

It is not at all easy to place Benjamin's view regarding the relative merits of original versus translation against the background I have briefly sketched. For Benjamin cannot be seen as a spokesman for either "adequacy" or "acceptability". On the one hand, literal translation and "breaking through the rotten barriers" of the target language make reading troublesome and rule out popular "acceptability" in the target culture; on the other hand, the irrelevance of equivalent meaning and similarity to Benjamin's concept of translation makes "adequacy" impertinent. "[...] no translation would be possible", he says, "if, in accord with its ultimate essence, it were to strive for similarity to the original" (2012, p. 77). "For in its continuing life," he adds, "which could not be so called if it were not *the transformation and renewal of a living thing*, the original is changed" (ibid., my italics).

This concept of translation as the "Fortleben", continuing life, of the original – the process of advance and perfection that we saw earlier – seems to support the pre-eminence of translation over original. For doesn't Benjamin define the translator's task as "bringing the seeds of pure speech to maturation in translation" and making the original grow into "a linguistic sphere that is both higher and purer"? (pp. 80, 79).

The starting-point of the original's "Fortleben" is, as we have seen, a literal translation which conveys word and syntax rather than meaning. Meaning is a wall that blocks the light of the original, whereas word-for-word rendering is an "arcade" that lets it through. Thus, the progressive advance of the original text towards its "Adamic" version is a gradual gain of "pure speech" and a gradual loss of meaning. As such, literal translation according to Benjamin is the very opposite of what it is to his 19th and early 20th century predecessors: a return to the original not in order to fathom its meaning, but to uncover its poetic essence and "bring its seeds of pure speech to maturation."

At the same time, Benjamin's image of the original and its various translations as so many fragments of a vessel seems to attribute to them all a similar standing, as the "fragments of a greater language". Neither the original nor any one of its translations can attain the "Pure Language" which is the entire vessel. This can be attained "only by the totality of their mutually complementary intentions" (p. 78). Nevertheless, even a single translation can be said to excell the original: for although only the utopian sum total of original plus all its translations can be said to attain Pure Language itself, every single translation contributes to the "continuing life" of the original by distilling from it the hidden, incommunicable, poetic residue of God's word.

Chapter Six

The Colloidal Suspension

The translator may misread his model in a number of ways; he may not see what is to be seen nor hear what is to be heard in it. But if he does see and hear clearly and fully, he will hold the original poem in a sort of colloidal suspension in his mind – I mean a fluid state in which the syntax, all the rigid features of the original dissolve, and yet its movements and inner structures persist and operate. It is out of these that he must make another poem that will speak, or sing, with his own voice. (Mathews, p. 67)

If in the original, content and language constitute a certain unity, like that between a fruit and its skin, a translation surrounds its content, as if with the broad folds of a royal mantle. For translation indicates a higher language than its own and thereby remains inadequate, violent and alien with respect to its content. (Benjamin 2012, p. 79)

Both mottoes to the present chapter deal with what is kept and what is discarded in translation. The first says the syntax and rigid features dissolve, whereas the "movements and inner structures" persist. The second says that what is lost (for good or bad, as we shall see) is the unity of content and language, but each of the two elements, though now separate, persists. The first deals with the translator and what he does when he transforms the original poem into another poem; the second – with the texts themselves, original and translated, and how they differ from each other. The first is by Jackson Mathews, an American translator of French poetry, the second by Benjamin.

The first quotation is obviously written by a traditional translator of the "acceptability" school, who believes the translation of a poem to be "another poem" which "speaks or sings with the translator's own voice". The syntax as well as other "rigid features" dissolve, for the translator's aim is not to produce an "adequate" translation; he wants to make another poem in his own voice, that is a voice acceptable to contemporary readers. At the same time, it should be a poem that reproduces the "movements and inner structures" of the original.

The distinction between "rigid features" and "inner structures", though easy to accept, is far from simple. Are run-on lines, for instance, a "rigid feature" or an "inner structure"? And what about rhyme? and metaphor? Should the original rhyme-pattern, or run-on design, dissolve in translation or persist and operate?

All such questions may be said to amount to one major question: what is the nature of the "colloidal suspension" that the translator's mind holds as it moves from original to translation? Mathews' image, the "colloidal suspension", is suggestive, calling to mind gelatin, fluid but resilient, mediating between the solid stuff of its origin and that of its product, between the original poem and the translated one. But what does this gelatin extract from the original and pass on to the translation – meaning or music? sense or sound? reference or connotation? signifier or signified? either? neither?

The sound and music of words, their materiality, cannot be transposed from one language to another. "The materiality of a word", to quote Jacques Derrida, "cannot be translated or carried over into another language. Materiality is precisely that which translation relinquishes. To relinquish materiality: such is the driving force of translation" (Derrida 1978, p. 210). Hence, the common translator would say that the signified meaning, sense, or reference, is what the "colloidal suspension" consists of. It may also include material features such as rhyme, but only inasmuch as they contribute to the meaning. If translation, to quote again its popular definition from Wikipedia, is "the communication of the meaning of a source- language text by means of an equivalent target-language text", it is meaning that the "colloidal suspension" retains and passes on to the target-language text. Translation, according to its classical concept, consists, to quote John Sallis, "in the movement from a unit in one language (word, phrase, sentence, etc.) to a corresponding unit in the other language, this movement being carried out by way of circulation through the signification, the meaning [...] a translation is true to its original if it has the same meaning. The measure of translation is restitution of meaning" (Sallis, pp. 63–64). The post-Romantic translator would add that meaning can never be left virgin in translation, and that the transposition of meaning is modified by the "play of the imagination" which transforms, not only transposes, the original. This transformation must remain, however, regulated by meaning (ibid. p. 107). Meaning remains the main and indispensable component of the "colloidal suspension".

But what happens when translation, as in Benjamin, is not primarily regulated by meaning? When the affinity between original and translation is not similarity of meaning? When it is the "kinship" between languages, their being fragments of a larger language, that connects original and translation? When it is their joint progress towards "Pure Language", towards Truth, or Revelation, beyond signification by any single language, that combines original and translation?

John Sallis' discussion of this problem deserves to be quoted in full (pp. 107–111), but we must make do with one central passage. For all its radicality, says Sallis, Benjamin's omission of meaning from the translation process –

> does not break entirely with the classical determination of translation. In the end [...] Benjamin's analysis invokes pure meaning such as would remain uncontaminated by signifying operations. This pure meaning, virgin and untouched, is no longer (as in the classical determination) that which can be said (signified) in any particular language but rather is, in a very classical sense, the ideal, that which all languages together, with their mutually supplementary intentions, would say if that totality of significa-tion were, at the limit, to be realized. Thus, Benjamin's analysis posits at the ideal limit a totality of meaning that would have escaped contami-nation by signification, a realm of meaning in which all communication and even all intentions are extinguished, a pure language in which there remains only the expressionless word. (pp. 109–110)

To Sallis, translation that aims at the pure, "expressionless" word which signifies nothing and is identical with Truth beyond all sense, cannot be regulated. "Could ripening the seed of pure language ever become – or be assured of becoming – a regulated transformation?", he asks (p. 110).

No, one agrees, it cannot; translation, if not completely arbitrary, cannot but be regulated by sense. But if equivalent sense is not its goal, if "completion", not similarity, is what it aims at, it must be regulated by means additional to sense and transcending sense. If the mystical task of the translator is to lead the original toward its ideal version, toward the ultimate, unsayable poem, part of the entire "vessel" and "Pure Language", the translator must follow rules other than that of equivalent sense. He must "fashion in [his] own language a counterpart to the original's mode of intention" (Benjamin 2012, p. 81) and thereby advance the translated text toward "Pure Language".

How is this to be done? Earlier, we quoted an example from Hölderlin's *Antigone*, mainly to stress the difficulty of exempting translation from regulation by meaning. In the next chapter, following another example quoted by Berman – Paul Celan's translation of a poem by Supervieille – I shall describe two attempts at answering the question of translation-unregulated-by-meaning, one by Peter Szondi, the other by Paul de Man and Barbara Johnson. Szondi's answer is implied, rather than stated, by his discussion of another translation by Paul Celan, whereas de Man and Johnson approach it in a direct discussion of Benjamin's theory of translation itself.

Chapter Seven

Benjamin and Paul Celan's Way to Pure Language

In Chapter 4 above, having described Antoine Berman's discussion of a line from Sophocles in Hölderlin's literal translation, I mentioned his further example (borrowed from Steiner) of Paul Celan's translation of a poem by Supervieille. The original lines "Et le soupir de la Terre/ dans le silence infini" are rendered by Celan as "das Seufzen dieser Erde / im Raum, der sie umschweigt". Unlike Hölderlin's translation, this one is not literal. Instead, what it does, says Berman, is that "it *condenses* what remains loose and poetically poorly expressed in Supervielle's text [...] natural language suddenly becomes invested with a greater urgency [...] German blossoms to liberate the poetic intention imma-nent in the original" (Berman, pp. 157–158).

"Condensation", "Urgency", "Liberation" are, I feel, too abstract and vague to shed much light on the transition from French to German in this case, let alone on what Benjamin was trying to say about translation and its progress towards purity. I find Peter Szondi's discussion of another Celan translation more concrete and therefore more useful.

The Hungarian-born literary scholar Peter Szondi was a great admirer of Celan, and tragically followed him, committing suicide a year and a half after the latter's death. One of his last texts, which he planned to be included in a "petit bouquin sur Paul" (Szondi 1972, p. 9) was an article entitled "Poetry of Constancy – Poetik der Beständigkeit. Celans Übertragung von Shakespeares Sonett 105" (Szondi 1992). Although it deals with Celan's method of translation and only incidentally with Benjamin's theory of translation, it offers, I believe, one way of under-standing Benjamin and his theory.[12]

Before trying to show how, let me emphasize the basic difference, indeed opposition, between Celan's concept of poetry and that of Benjamin.

"No Reader" and "Inessential Meaning", to quote the titles of my Chapters 1 and 2, are inimical to Celan's idea of what poetry does and is expected to do. Poetry to Celan, on the contrary, is the presence of poet and reader, a dialogue and encounter with the other, not at all the Symboliste craving after pure "Kunst". "Should we think Mallarmé through to the end?", he asks, and his answer, though not stated, is clear enough; for a few pages later he sides with those poets "who do not forget that they speak from an angle of reflection which is their own existence" and commends the reader, the "other" whom the poet "intends" and "needs" (Celan, pp. 44, 49).[13] Mallarmé neither condescends to the angle of his own existence nor intends or needs the other.

In spite of the distance between Celan and Benjamin, however, Szondi detects in Celan's translation of Shakespeare's Sonnet 105, when compared with the English original, a shift in the "mode of intention" related to Benjamin's theory. "[...] Benjamin saw the legitimacy, indeed the necessity, of translating as lying in the different intentions toward language and modes of signification displayed by an original text and its translation", he writes (Szondi 1992, p. 168). In Celan's version of Shakespeare's sonnet, the "mode of signification" differs from that of the original in that constancy, the subject of the sonnet, "is not merely the intended meaning; it *characterizes the verse itself*" (p. 173, my italics).

How does constancy "characterize the verse itself"? By means of linguistic repetitions and similarities which embody *in language itself* the constancy which is only *spoken about* in Shakespeare's original. Szondi's brilliant analysis of how this is done is too intricate to be described here. One example should suffice. The chiastic structure of the original line "Kind is my love to-day, to-morrow kind" is given up in Celan's version: "Gut ist mein Freund, ists heute und ists morgen". Instead of Shakespeare's line which only declares its content, enclosing the flow of time in an irrelevant chiastic structure ("kind-today-tomorrow-kind"), Celan embodies content in form, enacting both the flow of time and the constancy which overrules it by means of a threefold repetition: "ist – ists – ists".

Szondi sums up: In "Shakespeare's original [...] constancy is *sung about and described*; in Celan, constancy is realized *in verse*." (pp. 179–180, my italics).

Going back to our question concerning the way translation is supposed, according to Benjamin, to lead the way to the ultimate poem in the "Pure Language", Szondi's implied answer seems to be that by advancing from the referential to the poetic use of language, from discursive to non-discursive, translation can bring the translated text closer to Mallarmé's "immortal word" (Mallarmé 1897, p. 242) which is always silent. In this case it may be said to be regulated, not only by the sense itself, but by the "mode of intention" toward language, the "mode of signification that stamps linguistic usage" (Szondi 1992, p. 167, n.5). The mode of signification that regulates Celan's Shakespeare translation would be the embodiment of sense in form, the "poetic" mode of signification.

Szondi's implied interpretation of Benjamin's method makes good sense in that it shows it to be a process of upgrading in the poetic quality of the translated text. If translation is supposed to centre, not on the "inessential" message, but on the "incomprehensible, the secret, the 'poetic'" (Benjamin 2012, p. 75), Celan's transformation of Shakespeare's sonnet from referential to poetic, from "constancy sung about and *described*" to "constancy *realized in verse*" is a convincing example of this supposition. Szondi also relates Celan's strategy, particularly his many repetitions, to Roman Jakobson's principle of "equivalence" realized in the "poetic function" of language, thus enhancing the poetic element in Celan's translation as well as in Benjamin's theory (pp. 182–3)[14].

In the last analysis, however, Szondi admits that Jakobson's "poetic function" of language "can never be fully realized", because equivalence, when "promoted to the constitutive device of the sequence", must end in tautology if the poem "is to say anything at all" (p. 183). This is the cul-de-sac of meaninglessness that Benjamin speaks about, the translator's being "locked up in silence" (2012, p. 83). But Benjamin, as we shall see, goes one mystical step further and ends with the Truth beyond meaning.

Paul de Man, in a lecture at Cornell University in 1983 entitled "Conclusions: on Walter Benjamin's 'The Translator's Task' ", offers a deconstructive reading of Benjamin which may be said to be diametrically opposed to Szondi's. Barbara Johnson largely follows his reading in a chapter on Benjamin's essay included in her book *Mother Tongues*. If to Szondi, translation à la Benjamin is the promotion of a text, to de Man and Johnson it is its disintegration. In his "Des Tours de Babel", Derrida writes:

> [...] if the original calls for a complement, it is because at the origin it was not there without fault, full, complete, identical to itself. From the origin of the original to be translated there is fall and exile. (Derrida 1985, p. 188)

De Man follows suit: translation "shows in the original a mobility, an instability, which at first one did not notice" (de Man p. 82). Like critical philosophy or like literary theory as de Man the deconstructionist sees it, translation "[undoes] the original", "[reveals] an essential failure, an essential disarticulation which was already there in the original" (p. 84). Translation, in de Man's most radical formulation, "[kills] the original, by discovering that the original was already dead" (ibid.) The task of the translator, says Szondi, is to advance the text *toward* (admittedly unreachable) wholeness; the task of the translator, de Man and Johnson say, is to underline the text's distance *from* wholeness.

How does the translator "discover that the original is already dead"? And where do de Man and Johnson find this rather upsetting idea in Benjamin's essay? Perhaps the best way of understanding this is by reference to Benjamin's words quoted as the second motto to our previous chapter: the two similes he uses to describe the relationship between language and content in the original and in the translation. "In the original," says Benjamin," content and language constitute a certain unity, like that between a fruit and its skin"; in a translation, on the other hand, language surrounds content "as if with the broad folds of a royal mantle". What the two similes seem to mean is rather conventional: that the original, unlike the translation, shows completeness, a unity of content and language, which is lost in translation (even though both persist). But to Barbara Johnson, Benjamin's similes mean the very opposite – revealed when the translator tries to achieve this presumable unity in his translation :

> the vessel seems whole in the original language only because the skin and the fruit have been produced together. Any translation immediately has to separate them. The appearance of wholeness is fragmented the moment the signifier and the signified are linked by the 'folds' of a

different system of differences. Blinded by the mirage of wholeness in the original language, the translator nevertheless has no choice but to fragment the vessel. The original reveals its illusion of wholeness to have already drawn on resources that were, at bottom, arbitrary. The work of art has simply found a way to make that arbitrariness work *for it*. The precarious appearance of unity was achieved by using the fortuitousness of the original language, but in any other language, such luck falls apart. (Barbara Johnson, p. 61)

The translator's task according to Benjamin, says Johnson, is to separate language from content, signifier from signified, and thus show their presumable unity in the original text to be illusory. According to Szondi, on the contrary, the translator's task is to bring language and content together, to embody in the language of the translation what was limited to content in the original. To de Man-cum-Johnson (but not to Derrida, as we shall see), every translation only breaks further what erroneously seemed like wholeness in the beginning; to Szondi, every translation brings us nearer to what, for Benjamin, was to be wholeness in the end.

Interestingly, however, Barbara Johnson too does not ignore the ultimate wholeness that Benjamin envisages :

Behind the diversity of languages shimmers a 'pure' vessel whose unity no one will ever piece together. *And yet, only translation can make it visible at all.* Humpty Dumpty's great fall creates the desire to put an egg back together again. But the wholeness translation reveals is not a restoration. The completion it points to is still – and perhaps forever, in human time – deferred. (p. 62, my italics)

Johnson does not believe that the ultimate wholeness really exists; she does not subscribe to any "Messianism". At the same time she does agree that "the piecing together of the fragments made visible by translation is structured *as if* [the ultimate wholeness] could [exist]" (ibid., my italics). Although we are not "progressing toward unity", and although "every effort to patch the vessel together only breaks it further", unity, indeed, "may well have existed in the beginning" (p. 64).

That is why the contrast between the two approaches is less cut and dried than it would seem. To de Man and Johnson, every translation only breaks further what seemed like wholeness in the beginning; to Szondi, every translation à la Benjamin brings us nearer to what will be wholeness in the end. But to Johnson no less than to Szondi, the whole, pure vessel "shimmers" behind the diversity of languages.

Paul de Man, Barbara Johnson and Peter Szondi all subscribe, in the last analysis, to Benjamin's belief that all that translation can and should do is to point toward the "inaccessible domain where languages are reconciled and fulfilled" (Benjamin 2012, p. 79). This ultimate domain remains "inaccessible" – "never fully realized" to Szondi (1992, p. 183), "forever deferred" to de Man and Johnson (Barbara Johnson, p. 64). At this point beyond sense, a point of total silence, structuralist poetics and deconstruction strangely shake hands.

Benjamin, however, as we have seen, does not stop short at that point. He concludes his essay with the Holy Scriptures, where language and Truth are united in the "True Language", and the flow of language, without the mediation of sense, is one with the flow of revelation. To attempt a definition of "Pure Language" in the sense of " True Language" will be our next task.

Chapter Eight

Pure Language

"Breaking through the rotten barriers" of language, which has often been regarded as the translator's means to enrich and expand his own language, is given, as we have seen, a far greater, utopian role in Benjamin's theory. The Benjaminian translator, writes George Steiner, "enriches his tongue by allowing the source language to penetrate and modify it. But he does far more: he extends his native idiom towards the hidden absolute of meaning" (Steiner, p. 65). This absolute of meaning – or rather of meaninglessness – is Pure Language which Benjamin derived partly, as Steiner briefly points out, from the Kabbalistic and Gnostic tradition (ibid., pp. 60–65).

I say "meaninglessness" because Benjamin's translation process, as we have seen, involves a gradual liberation from the bondage to "inessential" meaning. The irrelevance of meaning or message to Pure Language, which is the translator's final and unreachable goal, shows once again the influence of the Kabbalistic tradition with which Scholem acquainted Benjamin. To the Kabbalists, writes Scholem,

> the fact that God expressed Himself, even if His utterance is far beyond human insight, is far more important than any specific 'meaning' that might be conveyed. So considered, the Torah is an absolute and has primacy over all human interpretations, which, however deep they may penetrate, can only approximate the absolute 'meaninglessness' of the divine revelation. (Scholem 1965, p. 43)

The "absolute meaninglessness of the divine revelation", or God's creative word, must be distinguished, however, from the human, Adamic language, which, as we have seen, names God's nameless creation. "God made things knowable in their names", but it is man that "names them according to knowledge", says Benjamin in "On Language as such and on the Language of Man". Man, he says, "is the knower in the same language in which God is creator". Man translates the nameless into name, or the knowable into the known. Though this Adamic language was lost with the Tower of Babel, and its superior immediacy was replaced by the inferior mediateness of our common, communicative speech, it shares with the latter its cognitive nature and is not exempt, as is the creative language of God, from the "mediation of sense". It is only the meaningless absolute of divine revelation that can be regarded as the Pure Language proper.

The exclusion of meaning, thus, must be a major consideration in the search for the nature of Pure Language. And since meaning-making – and by implication, meaning-unmaking – belongs to semiotic studies, let us ask in semiotic terms: is Pure Language a language of mere signifieds? mere signifiers? Neither?

That the Pure Language, as the (utopian) end-product of translation, should consist of signifieds free from their signifiers would seem to be the obvious case. For isn't it the evident task of the translator, as we usually view it, to retain the signified while leaving its original signifier behind? Isn't his task to find a new signifier for the old signified? And, in terms of Benjamin's metaphysics, advancing from one single language to another on the way to the ultimate language, shouldn't all single signifiers be left behind on behalf of the pure signified?

Schopenhauer, to take a prominent (and anachronistic) example, would have answered in the positive. It is the *idea* expressed by the original text that has, according to Schopenhauer, "to be dissolved into its most basic components and then reconstructed in the new language". Or again: "the translation into Latin often requires a breakdown of a sentence into its most refined, elementary components (the *pure thought* component) from which the sentence is then regenerated in totally different forms" (Schopenhauer, pp. 33–35).

There is no need, however, to remind ourselves that the idea, or the pure thought component, is not what Benjamin takes the Pure Language to consist of. It is, on the contrary, "something other than the reproduction of meaning" that he expects translation to promote. Meaning liberated from its signifier is not his concept of Pure Language – a language which is "the meaningless absolute of the divine revelation".

If so, does it consist, on the contrary, of signifiers free from signifieds? Does the translator "integrate the plurality of languages into a single true language" by eliminating signification, by liberating words from their signifying function?

A word that does not signify is pure materiality, pure sound, and that is precisely what cannot be transposed from one language to another. Benjamin, therefore, cannot possibly mean Pure Language to consist of the pure sound of words. What he wants translation's language to do, having freed itself from "bondage to the sense", is, as we have seen, "to allow its own mode of *intentio* to resound". And the mode of intention, as distinct from the intended content, is the hardly definable way in which the referent "bread", for instance, is signified by "pain" in French versus "Brot" in German. This is the "poetic significance" of the sense of a word, a significance "not exhausted by what the word means, but rather achieved precisely through the way in which what is meant is bound up with the mode of meaning in the particular word" (2012, p. 80). This rather tortuous definition is then reduced to two simple words: " It is customary to express this by saying that words carry *emotional connotations*" (ibid., my italics.) If translation liberates the signifier from its signified, it retains, even promotes, the "poetic significance" of the latter, its "emotional connotations".

If translation's aim, therefore, is to "integrate the plurality of languages into a single true language", it does so by transferring, not the signifieds of the translated text, but their emotional connotations. And Benjamin's assumption seems to be that not only words and phrases have their individual mode of meaning or emotional connotations, but an entire language is marked by a collective mode of intention, and that through translation the plurality of collective modes of intention may be integrated into a total mode that would characterize Pure Language itself. The combined modes of intention of "bread", "Brot", "pain", "pan", "pane" etc. would make up the "mode of intention" of the object "bread" in the Pure Language, just as the collective modes of intention of English, German, French, Italian, Spanish etc. etc. – "the totality of their mutually complementary intentions" (2012, p. 78) – would combine to create the Pure Language. This is how Derrida puts it in *Des Tours de Babel*:

> Through each language something is intended which is the same and yet which none of the languages can attain separately. They can claim, and

> promise themselves to attain it, only by coemploying or codeploying their intentional modes [...] Every 'thing', in its presumed self-identity (for example, bread *itself*) is intended by way of different modes in each language and in each text of each language. It is among these modes that the translation should seek, produce or reproduce, a complementarity or a 'harmony' [...] Owing to translation, in other words to this linguistic supplementarity by which one language gives to another what it lacks, and gives it harmoniously, this crossing of languages assures the growth of languages, even that 'holy growth of language' 'unto the messianic end of history'. (Derrida 1985, pp. 201–202)

But does translation really assure the growth of language "unto the messianic end of history"? Does it actually reach to the ultimate Pure Language beyond its Adamic knowable version, beyond both meaning and intention? Let me quote John Sallis once more:

> Benjamin's analysis invokes pure meaning such as would remain uncontaminated by signifying operations. This pure meaning, virgin and untouched, is no longer (as in the classical determination) that which can be said (signified) in any particular language but rather is, in a very classical sense, the ideal, that which all languages together, with their mutually supplementary intentions, would say if that totality of signification were, at the limit, to be realized. Thus, Benjamin's analysis posits at the ideal limit a totality of meaning that would have escaped contamination by signification, a realm of meaning in which all communication and even all intentions are extinguished, a pure language in which there remains only the expressionless word. (Sallis, pp. 109–110)

Sallis' position remains on the "meaning" plane; he speaks of "pure *meaning* uncontaminated by signifying operations" and "a realm of *meaning* in which all communication and even all intentions are extinguished" (my italics). If Pure Language is a "realm of meaning", it retains, as Sallis has it, "a vestige of pure meaning", "even if at an unbridgeable distance" (ibid., p. 110). It must be regulated by meaning, by "that which the speech or [linguistic] work makes manifest". The "dream of pure language" devoid of signification "is also a dream of nontranslation" (ibid).

Benjamin, however, in the enigmatic conclusion to his essay, adds to language and meaning a third agent – Truth, or Doctrine, or Revelation, the exclusive realm of Holy Scripture. In Holy Scriptures' True

Language, sense no longer mediates between language and truth, sense "has ceased to be the watershed dividing the flow of language from the flow of revelation". The text there "belongs immediately to truth or doctrine, *without the mediation of the sense*"; it has the "literalness of the true language" (2012, p. 83., my italics). If in Hölderlin's Sophocles, the "harmony of languages is so deep" that meaning nearly disappears, in Holy Scriptures "language and revelation [are] united in the text", and the harmony of the original language and the translation language cannot disrupt revelation i.e. truth.

How can a text "belong immediately" to truth, "without the mediation of the sense"? Can the language of truth dispense with meaning?

I think the answer, considering the young Benjamin's historical position, must belong to theology. The various attempts to play down the theological nature of the conclusion to "The Translator's Task" seem problematic. Thus Paul de Man:

> [...] one is impelled to read *reine Sprache* as that which is the most sacred, which is the most divine, when in fact in Benjamin it means a language completely devoid of any kind of meaning function, language which would be pure signifier, which would be completely devoid of any semantic function whatsoever, a purely technical linguistic language – and it would be purely limited to its own linguistic characteristics. You can call that divine or sacred, if you want, but it is not mysterious in that sense, I think, though it is paradoxical in the extreme . . . (de Man, pp. 96–97)

It seems difficult to see this "extreme paradox" as making sense outside a religious framework. How can a language be "devoid of any semantic function" without being "mysterious"? Is calling it "divine or sacred" up to one's sweet will?

Another, more extended, attempt to avoid theology is made in the 10th Cahier of Antoine Berman's *The Age of Translation*. "Benjamin's Messianic framework makes Berman uncomfortable", says his translator Chantal Wright, and he argues, she says, that it "can be appropriated (or translated) into a more secular form" (Berman, p. 201). "For us", says Berman, as we "[move] away from the Messianic connotations that are historically peculiar to Benjamin", Pure Language is "language itself, in its existence-as-letter" (p. 205). Referring to Heidegger, he defines it as "language that is a non-signifying unfolding of the world", and therefore "natural" – the natural language "of *orality*" (pp. 206–207). Translation, he says, "happens in the *accentuation* of the orality present in the original. The attention paid to the *letter* is therefore inseparable from the attention paid to *orality* [...] Oral language is language itself. The ultimate definition of translation is that which frees the spark of orality within the original *written* text. [...] The passage from one language to another *can* free the oral from the written" (p. 208).

This Heideggerian emphasis on speech as the key to "Pure language", and as such to translation, seems open to question. How can the "interlinear version of the Holy Scriptures" be the "ideal of all translation", as Benjamin's says in the conclusion to his essay, if the ultimate definition of translation is "that which frees the spark of orality within the original written text"? Would Benjamin claim that the interlinear translation of the Holy Scriptures accentuates "the orality present in the original?"

Contrary to Berman, I don't believe one can "[move] away from the Messianic connotations that are historically peculiar to Benjamin". A meaningless text can express truth only if it *is* truth, and only revealed truth, the Holy Scriptures, can be said to be truth *notwithstanding its meaning*. Let us quote Scholem again on the Kabbalistic approach: "the fact that God expressed Himself, even if His utterance is far beyond human insight, is far more important than any specific 'meaning' that might be conveyed". And again, in "The Name of God and the Linguistic Theory of the Kabbala": "Here the Torah is conceived of as a mystical whole, whose purpose, in the first analysis, does not consist in conveying a specific message, but rather in giving expression to the power and almightiness of God himself" (1972, p. 79). It is revelation itself, the *event* of Revelation, not its *meaning*, that makes the Holy Scriptures the True Language. That is, I think, what Derrida means by "event" (événement):

> Transferability [traductibilité] pure and simple is that of the sacred text in which meaning and literality are no longer discernible as they form the body of a unique, irreplaceable, and untransferable [intransférable] event [...] It is the absolute text because in its event it communicates nothing, it says nothing that would make sense beyond the event itself. (Derrida 1985, pp. 203–204)

The "absolute text" is an event that communicates nothing beyond its being divine revelation. Benjamin concludes his essay with the following lines:

> [...] just as language and revelation must be united in the text, literalness and freedom must be united in the form of an interlinear translation. For to some degree all great writings, but above all Holy Scripture, contain their virtual translation between the lines. The interlinear version of the Holy Scriptures is the prototype or ideal of all translation. (p. 83)

What he means in this difficult passage is perhaps this: unlike Hölderlin's translations, which contribute to the "Fortleben" of Sophoclean tragedy by applying the Greek way of meaning to German, but thereby lose its meaning, the interlinear translation of the Holy Scriptures, likewise literal, cannot lose its meaning because it has no meaning. Its source language, being the True Language itself, needs no promotion, for its afterlife as Revelation is eternally secure; its target language, being a literal translation of the True Language, cannot lose its status as event rather than meaning. Thus, two extremes meet in the interlinear version of the Holy Scriptures: it is both literal and free, both subjected to language and exempted from the constraints of meaning. Being exempt from meaning, and nevertheless not being "locked up in silence", it is "the prototype or ideal of all translation". All translation strives to reach, in John Sallis's above-quoted words, "a pure language in which there remains only the expressionless word"; but this is no longer what he calls a realm of meaning but a realm of meaninglessness, or a meaningless event, superior, as God's Revelation, to all meaning.

Chapter Nine

Aura and Translation

"The Work of Art in the Age of Mechanical Reproduction" (Benjamin 1968, pp. 219–253)[15] is an essay Benjamin wrote in 1935 and published in 1936, that is, some twenty years after "On Language as Such and on the Language of Man" and fifteen years after "The Translator's Task". In the meantime he had made his much-discussed transition from theology to Marxism, "from a thought fed by theological intuitions to a vision of the world inspired by Marxism" (Mosès 2009, p. 67). In "The Work of Art in the Age of Mechanical Reproduction" one would thus expect him to abandon, if not oppose, the terms we discussed in connection with the earlier two essays. Moreover, what "The Work of Art" deals with is "mechanical reproduction", by which Benjamin means lithography, photography and film, not translation. The "mechanical" aspect of reproducibility, central to his discussion of contemporary art, is obviously irrelevant to literary translation.

If nevertheless I believe this late essay to have some interesting implications for the theory of translation, this is because Benjamin's discussion of "mechanical reproduction" shows some important common denominators with translation, in spite of the mechanical and clonish aspects of it.

Thus, both reproduction and translation suffer a similar loss: they lose the uniqueness and distance of their original. "Even the most perfect reproduction of a work of art", says Benjamin, "is lacking in one element: its presence in time and space, its unique existence at the place where it happens to be" (p. 222). The same may be said of the "most perfect" translation of a text: an original text, like an original work of art, belongs to a certain time and space, and exists uniquely "at the place where it happens to be", which is between the pages of the original text; its translation must necessarily lose this unique presence.

Translation, like reproduction, loses the authenticity of the original –

for "the presence of the original is the prerequisite to the concept of authenticity"; and since authenticity "is the essence of all that is transmissible from [an object's] beginning", including "its testimony to the history which it has experienced", "what is really jeopardized when the historical testimony is affected is the authority of the object" (pp. 222–223). As for translation, the authenticity and authority of an original text may be likewise said to be "really jeopardized" in its various translations. If the history of the 'Mona Lisa' "[...] encompasses the kind and number of its copies made in the 17th, 18th, and 19th centuries" (p. 245 n.1), the same can be said, for instance, of the history of the *Iliad* and *Odyssey*. Their numerous translations during those centuries lack the authority of the Greek original and drastically affect our concept of Homer.

What it all amounts to is the disintegration of what Benjamin calls the "aura" of the original: "that which withers in the age of mechanical reproduction is the aura of the work of art" (p. 223). Aura, as defined one page later, is "the unique phenomenon of a distance, however close it may be" (p. 224). That is, however physically close to the spectator (or reader) the reproduction (or translation) may be, the spectator/reader, contemplating it aesthetically, discovers something infinitely distant – not only in space or time, but, as Stéphane Mosès says, in the dimension of the imagination (Mosès 2003, p. 87). The aura of the Greek Homer cannot but disappear in e.g. a modern English translation, faithful as it may be to the form and content of the original.

That which destroys the aura of the original in modern times has to do with the "increasing significance of the masses in contemporary life", and it rests on two circumstances: "the desire of contemporary masses to bring things 'closer' spatially and humanly, which is just as ardent as their bent toward overcoming the uniqueness of every reality by accepting its reproduction" (p. 225).

Although the latter circumstance may not apply to translation, which derives from the lack of knowledge of the original language rather than out of a "bent toward overcoming uniqueness", the former certainly does. The possibility, if not desire, to bring the text closer to the reader, has always been open to the translator. Translation since Roman times, as we saw earlier, was regarded as a process of perfection rather than mere transmission, and perfection meant, not just perfecting one's target language by means of the source language, but also perfecting the original by putting the new life of the target language into it. The latter was defined by Schleiermacher, as seen above, as "[leaving] the reader alone as much as possible and [moving] the writer toward the reader". That is exactly what the "contemporary masses" expect according to Benjamin: to move the *Mona Lisa* toward them, or – if applied to translation – to do the same with the *Iliad* and *Odyssey*.

For the Marxist Benjamin, the decline of the aura which was based on ritual, and the elimination of distance and tradition, meant that "for the first time in world history, mechanical reproduction emancipate[d] the work of art from its parasitical dependence on ritual" (p. 226). Authenticity was no longer applicable to artistic production, and "the total function of art [was] reversed. Instead of being based on ritual, it[began] to be based on another practice – politics" (ibid.).

The new-found emancipation from ritual and religion, however, did not eliminate the yearning for the lost aura. In his late essay "On some Motifs in Baudelaire" (1939) (Benjamin 1968, pp. 157–202), as well as in "The Work of Art in the Age of Mechanical Reproduction", Benjamin "constantly contrasts the notion of a 'modern beauty' peculiar to the forms of art produced by new techniques of reproduction with the ideal of the disappeared auratic beauty" (Mosès 2009, p. 81). Creating a work of art, to Benjamin, remains in the last analysis basically different from the creation of a photograph: if photography is like food for hungry eyes, a painting is that which the same eyes "will never have their fill" of (Benjamin 1968, p. 189). This infinite plenitude or aura, disintegrated in "the experience of shock" of the modern city and its crowd, is the price Baudelaire paid in order to have "the sensation of the modern age" (p. 196).

Those who, unlike Baudelaire, refused to pay that price were the adherents of the doctrine of *l'art pour l'art*, and above all Mallarmé. Sensing the approaching crisis brought about by reproducibility, sensing that "the bourgeoisie [was seeking] to take its 'cause' from the hands of the writers and the poets" (Benjamin 1983, p. 106) they "reacted with the doctrine of *l'art pour l'art*', that is, with a theology of art. This gave rise to what might be called a negative theology in the form of the idea of 'pure' art [...]" (1968, p. 226). In Mallarmé and the theory of *poésie pure*, "the cause of his own class has become so far removed from the poet that the problem of a literature without an object becomes the centre of discussion. This discussion takes place not least in Mallarmé's poems, which revolve about *blanc, absence, silence, vide*" (1983, p. 106). Baudelaire, on the other hand, does not believe in autonomous art; his works "are not esoteric"; they reflect social experiences, particularly those of the big-city dweller (ibid.).

Following Stéphane Mosès, we earlier described Benjamin's early two essays as forming two contrary movements: "On Language as Such and on the Language of Man" presenting "human history as a process of decline", while "The Translator's Task" "describes it as a progress toward a utopian fulfillment". We also quoted Mosès to the effect that the two contrary movements combine "to trace the curve of original sin, and Fall, followed by a process of purification and progress toward renewal".

"The Work of Art in the Age of Mechanical Reproduction" seems to suggest a similar combination, though applied to reproducibility rather than translation, and, above all, exempt from theological categories. The Work of Art, either verbal or visual, undergoes a process of decline when reproduced – and, I claim, also when translated, – losing its aura, and thereby its uniqueness, authenticity and authority. In the two youthful essays, the aura belonged to Adamic language, was lost as a result of sin, and deteriorated to a mere instrument of communication. Decline in this context, taking place as a continuum of transformations or "translations", leads to "the abyss of the mediateness of all communication, of the word as means, of the empty word, [...] the abyss of prattle" (Benjamin 1979, p. 120).In the late essay, the aura belongs to art rather than language, and its loss has to do with the cultural revolution of the masses, who want closeness rather than distance and usefulness rather than uniqueness – or, as Joel Snyder has it, are "fundamentally opposed to the individual and irreproducible" (Snyder, p. 169). The liberation from religion and ritual, once regarded as a fall into an"abyss of prattle", has now become art's freedom"to be based on another practice – politics" (Benjamin 1968, p. 226).

Benjamin the Marxist cannot but celebrate this new-found freedom: "for the first time in world history, mechanical reproduction emancipates the work of art from its parasitical dependence on ritual" (ibid.). Politicizing art is the Communist response to the Fascist aestheticizing of politics (ibid. p. 224), by which Benjamin "cannot mean that art should be put into the service of sloganeering", but that "art production [must be put] into the hands of the workers and allow them to show themselves the world they are in the process of making" (Snyder p. 171).

But there is, as we have seen, an element in this late essay, as well as in the later Baudelaire essay, that runs counter to the celebration of the decline of the aura, and, in a way, goes back to, or rather yearns for,the process toward purification of art – or language – which "The Translator's Task" had undertaken. The refusal to submit to the shock of the modern city, the cult of beauty of *l'art pour l'art* exempt from religious cult, may be seen as an analogue of the progress toward True Language which had followed language's decline according to "The Translator's Task".

Do "The Work of art in the Age of Mechanical Reproduction" and "The Translator's Task", thus, meet over the gap of the years and the radical turn Benjamin's thought had made in the meantime? On the one hand, they definitely do not: the former, celebrating the liberation from religious cult that the contemporary work of art enjoys, focuses on the removal of art away from its origins towards its most practical version, the political one; the latter (as well as the conclusion of "On the Language as Such and on the Language of Man") delineates a utopian return of art – or rather language – to its most non-communicative version in God's *Fiat*. Translation, in the light of the early two essays, departs from the original text towards the ultimate verbal purity; translation, as implied by the late essay, would leave the original text to become a verbal battle-ax.

The late essay too, however, as well as the Baudelaire essays, allude, as said before, to an opposite direction, that of *l'art pour l'art*: towards pure art, analogous to the True Language, though not only free from the older theology, but "relieved of any concern with nonartistic matters" (Snyder p. 168). This auratic direction is admittedly feeble and peripheral, "scattered traces of auratic experiences within modernity [...] 'slivers of messianic time' [which] are lost in a reality hopelessly emptied of all auratic magic" (Mosès, 2009, pp. 82–83). Hannah Arendt's following words, from her introduction to Benjamin's *Illuminations*, sum up what remains unchanged in Benjamin's approach:

> Whatever theoretical revisions Benjamin may subsequently have made in these theological-metaphysical convictions, his basic approach, decisive for all his literary studies, remained unchanged: not to investigate the

utilitarian or communicative functions of linguistic creations, but to understand them in their crystallised and thus ultimately fragmentary form as *intentionless and noncommunicative utterances of a 'world essence'*. (Benjamin 1968, p. 50, my italics).

Chapter Ten

Rosenzweig and Translation
Back Into Life

God is present, and if he acts through messengers, they are not postmen bringing yesterday's news, which perhaps in the meantime has already been overtaken by the intervening events; rather in this moment of theirs God is what acts immediately in them and speaks immediately through them. (Rosenzweig 1994, p. 42)

To walk humbly with thy God – the words are written over the gate, the gate that leaves out of the mysterious-miraculous light of the divine sanctuary in which no man can remain alive. Whither, then, do the wings of the gate open? Thou knowest it not? INTO LIFE. (Rosenzweig 1985, p. 424)

A year after the publication of Benjamin's "The Translator's Task", which accompanied his Baudelaire translations, another essay accompanying another body of translations followed: the German Jewish philosopher Franz Rosenzweig's "Afterword" to his German translation of poems by the twelfth-century Spanish Jewish poet Jehuda Halevi (1924). A year later, In the newly founded journal *Die Kreatur,* Rosenzweig published "Die Schrift und das Wort. Zur neuen Bibelübersetzung" ("Scripture and Word: On the New Bible Translation") – an introduction to the great translation project he had undertaken with Martin Buber, a new German translation of the Old Testament itself. Because of his fatal illness, and then his untimely death in 1929, Rosenzweig only managed to collaborate on the project up to the book of *Isaiah* chapter 53, and Buber completed it 36 years later, in 1961.

The question of Rosenzweig's influence on Benjamin cannot occupy us here. For our purpose it is enough to point out that, for chronological reasons, influence – with regard to the concept of translation – can be ruled out in the case of Benjamin's two youthful essays (Mosès 1989, p. 230).[16] At the same time, the deep affinity between the two thinkers' approach to translation is striking, as is the even deeper disparity between them.

As in Benjamin, language and world are one in Rosenzweig's major work, *The Star of Redemption* (1921). Language to Rosenzweig, as Stéphane Mosès puts it in his book on his philosophy, "constitutes the reality it designates", and he quotes Rosenzweig: "The world is never without the word. Indeed, it only exists in the word, and without the word there would be no world" (Mosés 1992, p. 151).

But this affinity with Benjamin hides a deeper disparity, as it emerges from the following lines from Rosenzweig's Afterword to Halevi's poems:

> That innovation in one language can happen by means of another language presumes of course that just as the language has given birth to each of its speakers, so all human speaking, all other languages ever spoken or to be spoken, are present in that one language at least in embryo. And this is the case. *There is only one language.* There is no linguistic peculiarity of one language that cannot be found contained, at least in embryo, in every other language, even if only in idioms, in nurseries, in jargons. The possibility of translating and the necessity of translating, the translator's Can, May and Shall are all founded on this essential unity of all language and the commandement of universal human communication based on that unity. (Buber & Rosenzweig, Preface p. lii, my italics).

The last lines may be said to sum up Rosenzweig's concept of translation in its affinity with, and crucial difference from, Benjamin's. The translator's "Shall" – what to Benjamin is his "Aufgabe" or task – depends, as in Benjamin, on the existence of an essential unity of all languages. Man, to quote Mosés, "lives utopia in a universal language that would unite all men beyond the specifity of their personal experiences" (1992, p. 120). But (a very considerable "but") the translator's task is not to lift language out of its inferior condition as an instrument of communication, as in Benjamin, but on the contrary, to contribute to "universal human communication".

Communication as the very *raison d'être* of language rather than the main symptom of its decadence is what sets Rosenzweig's idea of translation apart from Benjamin's. For if translation to Benjamin is motivated by a return to a mythic past and to Adamic language, in which word is identical with thing, not its arbitrary sign, to Rosenzweig it is meant to promote communication now, in man's dialogue with his fellow-men and his experience of dialogue with God. God's messengers (as in our motto to this chapter) are "not postmen bringing yesterday's news": God speaks "immediately through them".

"When seeking insight into a work of art or an art form, it never proves useful to take the audience into account": this opening sentence of Benjamin's "The Translator's Task" is the very opposite of Rosenzweig's approach. To the latter, the audience is the very life of the work of art:

> Who then will erect the bridge over which the work can move from its home-less isolation into a roomy, human home whence it can no longer be forcibly evicted, and where it meets many others of its own sort that permanently dwell together here in each other's company? This place where the works establish a broad, vital, enduring existence in beauty, and where the animation of the individual works themselves gradually animates an abundant whole of human life, *this place is the spectator.* (Rosenzweig 1985 p. 243, my italics)

To Benjamin, the exclusion of the audience opens the way to his subversive, mystical concept of translation, not as an event between text and audience, but as a cosmic happening between languages, which lifts them up from their diversity to the ultimate one language of Truth. To Rosenzweig too, the diversity of languages is a symptom of our unredeemed state: "Nothing shows so clearly that the world is unredeemed as the diversity of languages" (1985, p. 295). But if there is, as he says, "only one language", that language is not relegated to a mythic past, but detected in the very heart of diversity: "There is no linguistic peculiarity of one language that cannot be found contained, at least in embryo, in every other language, even if only in idioms, in nurseries, in jargons." The One Language, here too, may "in the last judgement" merge into God's totality,"the names of all into His nameless One" (p. 238); but the divine word, before it merges into his nameless totality, is not inaccessible to human speech:

> The ways of God are different from the ways of man, but the word of God and the word of man *are the same.* What man hears in his heart

as his own human speech is the very word which comes out of God's mouth[…] that word of creation which reverberates within us and speaks from within us – all this is also the word which God has spoken and which we find inscribed in the Book of the Beginning, in Genesis. (p. 151, my italics)

If the translator's resulting task is to detect the traces of the One Language in the idioms and jargons of the source language, and transfer – or embody, or re-invent – them into the target language, he must choose the *literal* method of translation. Instead of finding equivalent idioms or jargons in his own language without "breaking through its barriers", instead of making what is foreign acceptable to the target reader, he must transplant the original ones into his own language, thus Graecize his German like Hölderlin in his translations, or Hebreicize his German, like Buber and Rosenzweig himself in their Bible translation. Rudolf Pannwitz's approach, approved by Benjamin (and quoted above), is shared by Rosenzweig: "Our translations", says Pannwitz, "even the best –

start out from a false principle. They want to germanize Indic, Greek, English, instead of indicizing, graecizing, anglicizing German [...] the fundamental error of the translator is that he holds fast to the state in which his own language happens to be rather than allowing it to be put powerfully in movement by the foreign language.

Asking whether such a violation of one's target language,"[reflecting] the foreign tone in its foreigness: not [Germanizing] what is foreign, but rather [making] foreign what is German", is at all possible, Rosenzweig answers:

The Germanization of what is foreign[…] is done in the German that is already there […] as a person speaks who has nothing to say. Since he has nothing to say, he does not need to demand anything of the language […] He who has something to say will say it in a new way. He becomes the creator of language. After he has spoken, the language has a different face from before.[…] the foreign poet calls into the new language not merely what he himself has to say, but rather he brings along with it the heritage of the general language-spirit of his language to the new language, so that here not merely a renewal of the language occurs through the foreign person, but rather through the foreign language-spirit itself. (Galli, pp. 170–171)

The foreignization of German through translation, as Rosenzweig understands it, is different from Benjamin's. Its goal above all is to enable German to express what it previously couldn't, and only implicitly to lead to the One Language. The translator becomes the creator *in his own language*, he renews it by introducing both a foreign voice and the general language-spirit that resides in it. The end, as in the perfection-through-translation maintained by the ancient Romans or by Pannwitz, is to make the *target* language a more flexible, more expressive instrument of communication. Translation has only indirectly to do with the ultimate redemptive harmonization of all languages.

At the same time, the very fact that language x may be perfected by the import of elements from language y, shows the basic affinity between languages, and, ultimately, it shows that " there is only one language". The essential unity of all languages is, as we have seen, the basic common denominator of Rosenzweig's and Benjamin's theory of translation; except that " the commandement of universal human communication based on that unity" sets the former radically apart from the latter. Instead of breaking through the "rotten" barriers of German, it broadens its communicative reach by importing into German the sentence construction of, for instance, Hebrew (in Luther's Bible), "conquering for the realm of contemporary German the new province of Bible-German" (Galli, p. 172). Unlike the silence that ultimately encompasses God's words in Benjamin's utopian return through translation to Pure Language, the Bible to Buber and Rosenzweig is "a Voice in an existential, dialogic relationship between a divine I and a mundane Thou" (Jay, p. 10).

This "attempt to move from the level of abstract theological theory to direct *Lebenspraxis*" and use translation "as a means of restoring a lost religious immediacy" (Jay, p. 14) accounts for the very different character of Rosenzweig's "Afterword" from Benjamin's "Translator's Task". If the latter (together with the earlier "On Language as such") delineates above all a mystical circular narrative, the former is a sober, primarily technical treatment of translation as praxis. When it comes to Halevi and medieval Jewish poetry, the problem of translation is "first of all quite simply an external problem of form" (Galli, p. 173). There follows a discussion of rhyme (the author humbly confessing his own use of "Mr. Spetutat's dictionary of rhyming words") and metre ("Here lies a really marked foreignness"). Next, the content (mainly the problem of the German reader's lack of knowledge of the Bible) and the choice of words ("He must reproduce word for word as they are given to him") are briefly discussed.

Rosenzweig is obviously more interested in the concrete aspects of the practice of poetry translation than is Benjamin, and hence his writings related to translation may superficially prove more useful for the poetry translator's actual practice. Our final objective, however, will be to see whether Benjamin's mystical approach, too, can be expected to have helpful implications for that common translator. Before that, however, Derrida's interesting – and problematical – adoption of Benjamin's theory must be looked into.

Chapter Eleven

Derrida and the King's Untouchable Body

[…] Benjamin notes […] that 'the language of the translation envelops its tenor like a royal cape with large folds' […] The king has indeed a body […] but this body is only promised, announced and dissimulated by the translation […] what counts is what comes to pass under the cape, to wit, the body of the king […] around which a translation busies its tongue, makes pleats, molds forms, sews hems, quilts, and embroiders. But always amply floating at some distance from the tenor. (Derrida 1985, pp. 193–194)

The above-quoted lines from Jacques Derrida's long essay *Des Tours de Babel* (1985), elaborating as they do on Benjamin's metaphor of the king's royal cape from "The Translator's Task", are one instance of Derrida's general method in this text. It is a commentary or elaboration on Benjamin's essay, which, while commenting on it, develops its author's own thoughts on translation. Thus, it goes back to our discussion of "The Translator's Task", while leading us on to a later version of the metaphysics of translation.

Although Derrida discusses, or touches on, translation in many of his works, I shall limit myself for clarity's sake to *Des Tours de Babel*, supplementing it with some autobiographical material from the later book *Le monolinguisme de l'autre* (1996), which in a way may be said – perhaps because of its personal viewpoint – to contribute particularly creative thoughts to the metaphysics of translation. The different starting-points of the two texts – Benjamin's essay on the one hand, Derrida's Jewish-Maghreb background on the other – account for the different directions they take.

Benjamin's simile of the royal cape, which can float around the king's body only "at some distance" (in Derrida's above-quoted words), is used, as we have seen, to describe the relationship between language and content in translation. The relationship between the two in the original, on the other hand, is like that between a fruit and its skin. To Barbara Johnson, the presumable unity between fruit and skin in the original must be separated by translation, "the appearance of wholeness [being] fragmented the moment the signifier and the signified are linked by the 'folds' of a different system of differences" (Barbara Johnson p. 61). What erroneously seemed like wholeness in the beginning is broken by translation. But we also saw that Johnson, though (or because?) she is an orthodox deconstructionist, does not ignore a unity that "may well have existed in the beginning": "Behind the diversity of languages shimmers a 'pure' vessel whose unity no one will ever piece together".

The unity of the "pure vessel", which no one will ever piece together, is the equivalent of Derrida's king's body which can be "only promised". Unlike Barbara Johnson, however, Derrida does not seem to regard the relationship between fruit and skin in the original as illusory or erroneous. Instead, he points out the difference between the "fruit" and another term used by Benjamin, the "essential core". The essential core, Benjamin says, is that in the original "which, in a translation, is more than a message", is beyond communication and untranslatable (2012, p. 79). While in Benjamin the distinction between "core" and "fruit" is rather vague, to Derrida –

> It is not certain that the essential 'core' and the 'fruit' designate the same thing. The essential core [...] is [... the] adherence between the tenor and the language, between the fruit and the skin. This may seem strange or incoherent (how can a core be situated between the fruit and the skin?). It is necessary no doubt to think that the core is first the hard and central unity that holds the fruit to the skin, the fruit to itself as well; and above all that, at the heart of the fruit, the core is 'untouchable', beyond reach and invisible. (Derrida 1985, p. 193)

The separation between the "core" and the "fruit", and the definition of "core" as that which "holds the fruit to the skin", is an important contribution to the theory of translation. Derrida puts his finger on what Benjamin referred to as "a certain unity" (2012, p. 79), and Szondi and Barbara Johnson called "wholeness". The untranslatable or untouchable element in translation, according to Derrida, is not just the *unity* of content and language, but the *glue* that makes them one. "Bread" is translatable, but the adhesive that makes the English word "bread" (or the German "Brot", or the French "pain" etc. etc.) adhere to its referent remains unknown and untouchable. This adhesive is close to Benjamin''s "Art des Meinens", or way of meaning, which differentiates the German "Brot" from the French "pain" even though their referent is the same (p. 78). That which separates "Brot" from "pain" is neither fruit nor skin, neither signified nor signifier, but a third element, the "core" or mysterious adherence between them. It is this third element that is untranslatable.

Translation, nevertheless, makes it emerge. Source language and target language intend the same referent, but can only (partly) reach it by co-operating, by "plying, replying, co-deploying of intentions" or of "cores"; for "through each language, something is intended that is the same and yet that none of the languages can attain separately." (Derrida 1985, p. 221). Translation, by activating such "co-deployment" of languages, pushes them toward a whole, ultimately intending to attain what Derrida at this stage still calls "pure language" beyond all individual languages; later on, as we shall see, he will deny its existence. "As long as this accord does not take place, the pure language remains hidden, concealed, immured in the nocturnal intimacy of the 'core'. Only a translation can make it emerge" (p. 222).

Benjamin's "pure language" is thus envisaged as the emergence of the "core" from its hiding-place in the individual language. As such, it remains ever unattainable or "deferred". At the same time, owing to translation, the "cores" that the target language lacks pass on to it "harmoniously" from the source language, so that "this crossing of languages assures the growth of languages, even" – Derrida notably adds – "that 'holy growth of language' 'unto the messianic end of history' " (pp. 201–202); notably – because Derrida seemed to have avoided theological terms up to this point, whereas now he declares "the sacred text" to be "the absolute text", the embodiment of "pure" language, "because in its event it communicates nothing, it says nothing that would make sense beyond the *event* itself" (pp. 203–204, my italics). As suggested earlier, it is the *event* of Revelation, not its meaning, that seems to constitute the true language according to Derrida: he cannot but resort to theological terms when it comes to the "meaningless" language beyond all languages; "this religious code is essential here" (p. 202).

Thus, Derrida's general bent in this book follows Benjamin's. Like Benjamin, he reverses the old hierarchy of original translation, bestowing upon translation the capacity to ensure the "Fortleben", or survival, of the original through the harmonious crossing of languages, "even unto the messianic end of history". However – and this is a crucial point – Derrida's interpretation of the myth or figure of the Tower of Babel, which obviously relates to deconstruction – the philosophical "adventure" he is mainly known for – shows his elaboration of Benjamin to be rather problematic.

Deconstruction, by insisting that the accidental features of a text suvert its main message, that its message is ever irreferrable to reality and that there is nothing "outside the text", cannot but cancel the very possibility of metaphysics. In this sense, Derrida's *Des Tours de Babel* belongs to our study only in so far as Derrida follows Benjamin's myth of translation as a metaphorical support for his own deconstructive train of thought. The metaphor of the Tower of Babel is particularly relevant to his argument. The very title *Des Tours de Babel* combines tower, that is structure, with twists and turns (another meaning of "tour" in French), i.e. deconstruction. It exhibits two outcomes of the Babelian disaster: in addition to the multiplicity of tongues, as in Benjamin and as generally understood, also "an incompletion, the impossibility of finishing, of totalizing" (p. 165). The multiplicity of tongues makes translation necessary, while the confusion and incompletion makes it impossible. God "at the same time imposes and forbids translation" (p. 170).

As a result, Derrida's adoption of the Benjaminian concept of translation as conducive to the "holy growth of language", raises serious questions. Translation can hardly apply to a verbal text which constantly eliminates its own message. Benjamin too, we have seen, considered meaning inessential to translation, which had to do with the "Art des Meinens", not with the "Gemeinte". And Derrida, by adding the concept of the "core", saw it as untouchable, with translation always floating at some distance from it. But by destabilizing all components of language, deconstruction deprives its "rotten barriers" of the capacity to be broken through. It simply no longer *has* any barriers, but keeps differing and being deferred, keeps sliding and twisting, discarding one "fruit" for another, one core for another. If *différance* means that "the sign represents the presence in its absence", "takes the place of the present", and therefore is "deferred presence", "presence remains deferred in the translating text or rewriting just as it is deferred in the 'original'" (Kruger p. 52, quoting Derrida 1982, p. 9).

The division between translation and original, thus, loses its absolute status. The "growth" of the original by means of its translations becomes questionable. "From the origin of the original to be translated there is fall and exile", says Derrida, and "the translator must redeem, absolve, resolve [...]". His task, quoting Benjamin, is "to redeem in his own tongue that pure language exiled in the foreign tongue, to liberate by transposing this pure language captive in the work" (1985, *p.* 188). On the other hand, however, if the original shows "fall and exile", if It has no barriers to be broken through, if its way of meaning or core ever slides and differs, the "liberation" through translation of the Pure Language captive in it becomes untenable.

E.T. Bannet, in her article "The Scene of Translation: After Jakobson, Benjamin, de Man, and Derrida", claims that "after Derrida, it becomes apparent that [...] the failure of translation and the wandering, errance, and exile of language envelop two possibilities, one lethal, the other curative". Derrida, in his treatment of Benjamin's "The Translator's Task", develops, says Bannet, the "curative" possibility, while de Man develops the "lethal" one and believes translation not to relate to the life of the original, but to its death (Bannet, pp. 580–581).

What seems obvious from our discussion is that de Man (and Barbara Johnson) are more consistent, as deconstructionists, than their mentor. Instead of the translator as "redeemer", de Man brands him as a killer, destroying the original "by discovering that the original was already dead". Deconstruction – in spite of the endeavour to show that translation can be "curative" – cannot but underline its distance from the "Language of Truth".

Eleven years later, in *Monolingualism of the Other*, Derrida seems to have freed himself from Benjamin's authority. The small book is highly personal, and the ideas on translation are subjected to its autobiographical and political agenda. For all that, the way they emerge out of the personal memoir, and the quality they are lent thereby, are fascinating.

His starting-point is an "antinomy":

1. We only ever speak one language.
2. We never speak only one language. (1998, p. 7)

Or, in another version:

> I only have one language, yet it is not mine. (p. 2)

The one language, for a Franco-Maghrebian Jew like himself, is French. It is the only language he speaks, but it is not his. The only language he speaks, owing to the "coloniality of culture", is "the language of the other" (pp. 24–25). Paradoxically, however, he is barred access not only to Arabic and Berber, weakened, indeed forbidden, "by a colonial policy that pretended to treat Algeria as a group of three French departments" (p. 38), but also to French, forbidden "equally but differently" (p. 41):

> We only ever speak one language – and, since it returns to the other, it exists asymmetrically, always for *the other*, from the other, kept by the other. Coming from the other, remaining with the other, and returning to the other. (p. 40)

Thus, what is supposed to be one's mother tongue, French, has its "source, norms, rules, and law [...] situated elsewhere" (p. 41), representing the language of the master, a master who lives overseas (pp. 42–43). And in addition to the first and second interdicts, against Arabic and Berber and against French itself, the great majority of Maghrebian Jews are strangers to Jewish culture, "a strangely bottomless alienation of the soul" (p. 53).

Out of this complex situation, the "monolingualism of the other", a fascinating metaphysics of translation emerges above and beyond this particular situation:

> The monolingual of whom I speak speaks a language of which he is *deprived*. The French language is not his. Because he is therefore deprived of *all* language, and no longer has any other recourse – neither Arabic, nor Berber, nor Hebrew, nor any languages his ancestors would have spoken – because this monolingual is in a way *aphasic* (perhaps he writes because he is an aphasic), he is thrown into absolute translation, a translation without a pole of reference, without an originary language, and without a source language. For him there are only target languages [*langues d'arrivée*] [...] [which] no longer know where they are coming from, what they are speaking from and what the sense of their journey is [...] From these sole 'arrivals' [...] desire springs forth [...] to recon-

struct, to restore, but it is really a desire to invent a first language that would be, rather, a prior-to-the-first language destined to translate that memory. But to translate the memory of what, precisely, did not take place [...]. (pp. 60–61)

The Maghrebian Jew "is thrown into absolute translation" – absolute in the sense that it has no source language, only target languages. As a result, he desires to invent a "first language" into which he may translate what never took place.

The plight of the Franco-Maghrebian Jew is thus used to serve as a foundation for a metaphysical world-picture – or rather language-picture – that goes far beyond him, has, indeed, little to do with him. It equally applies, for instance, to the Jews of the Balkans and Eastern Europe. In a long endnote (no.9), Derrida expands his discussion to both sides of the Mediterranean, quoting Franz Rosenzweig's *The Star of Redemption* to the effect that the "eternal people" –

everywhere [...] speak the language of their external destinies, for example, the language of the people in whose dwelling place they reside as guests [...] they never possess this language on the grounds of their belonging to the same blood, but always as the language of immigrants who have come from everywhere [...] their linguistic life always feels (dis)located in an alien land, and [...] their personal linguistic fatherland is known to be elsewhere, in the sphere of the holy language, inaccessible to everyday speech. (pp. 79–80)

Derrida, thus, transcends his own background, using his "monolanguage of the other" and the lack of originary language as a counter-argument (or counter-myth) to Benjamin's ascent through translation to Adamic or Pure Language. Adamic Language, Derrida is saying, does not exist; it is a fictitious projection of the desperate need to escape the "text" that is our only home ("il n'y a pas de hors-texte"). There is no such thing as a pure language to escape to, nor does purity make sense: "I am from the very beginning attacking purity and purification" (p. 49). A philosophy such as the early Benjamin's or Rosenzweig's, that aims at a pure origin, is untenable from the deconstructive viewpoint:

As I do in all fields, I have never ceased calling into question the motif of 'purity' in all its forms (the first impulse of what is called 'deconstruction' carries it toward this 'critique' of the phantasm or the axiom of purity, or toward the analytical decomposition of a purification that would lead back to the indecomposable simplicity of the origin) […]. (p. 46)

Translation, therefore, reverses its direction: human language is no longer, as in Benjamin, the human *source* language from which we are required to climb towards its pure origin, but a *target* language, the only one possible, into which we delve in order to translate or haul the unknowable:

> […] everything that has, say, interested me […] could not not proceed from the strange reference to an 'elsewhere' of which the place and the language were unknown and prohibited even to myself, as if I were trying to *translate* into the only language and the only French Western culture that I have at my disposal, the culture into which I was thrown at birth, a possibility that is inaccessible to myself, as If I were trying to translate a speech I did not yet know into my 'monolanguage' […]. (p. 70)

Translating an unknown speech into a language which is "of the other" seems a doubly impossible task. Strangely enough, however, that unknown speech seems to be written, leave its traces, in "any given target language" (p. 65); "one must summon up writing inside the given language" (p. 64). The "writing" summoned up inside Derrida"s "monolanguage" cannot but be related to the "seeds of pure speech", dispersed in the plurality of languages, which, according to Benjamin, it is the translator's task to "bring to maturation in translation". Except that to Benjamin, this makes the original grow into "a linguistic sphere that is both higher and purer", while to Derrida what is written within language is invented, a phantasm projected by a "pre-originary language [that] does not exist" (p. 64).

In the last analysis, however, for all the diametrical opposition between "The Translator's Task" and "Monolingualism of the Other", both aspire to a lost origin and both entitle translation to lead us towards it. The early Benjamin conceives the origin in theological terms, conferring upon it truth and purity; the late Derrida, leaning on his autobiography, regards it as the projection of psychological discontent. The monolingual's deprivation throws him, he says, "into absolute translation" (p. 61): but what can "being thrown" mean except feeling the need for a "monolingualism of one's own", for an "absolute" language that would *not* "come from the other", *not* "remain with the other", and *not* "return to the other"?

Derrida's language-of-one's-own is as utopian as Benjamin's Pure Language. Both are unattainable, the former because there is no absolute origin in Derrida's world, the latter because Divine revelation is beyond our pale. It follows that translation, in either case, is deceptive and a failure: it never reaches its goal according to Benjamin, it has no source language according to Derrida.

Can their theories nevertheless shed some light on the translator's praxis? Can they be said to contribute anything to our understanding the task of translation?

Chapter Twelve

The Practical Dimension

> The practical dimension of Benjamin's text has been largely underestimated, probably because of the extremely speculative and at times theological character of certain arguments. Nevertheless, 'The Task of the Translator' remains a very practical text […]. (Weber, p. 55)

The question of the link between theory and practice in Benjamin's approach to translation has two separate aspects. On the one hand, one may ask whether his theory applies to his own practice, primarily to his Baudelaire translations. On the other hand, and more importantly, one wonders whether his theory is at all applicable to the practice of poetry translation as such, whether it can be said to have a "practical dimension", as Samuel Weber puts it.

Being an introduction to a translation of Baudelaire, one would expect "The Task of the Translator" to show at least an awareness of, if not focus on, the practical aspects of translating Baudelaire. Since it seems far from doing so, the link between "the Task" and the Baudelaire poems has often been ignored, or otherwise given rise to over-subtle, though sadly unconvicing, explanations. Thus, for instance, Caroline Sauter's book devoted to the connection between Benjamin's theory and his Baudelaire translations, is an illuminating commentary on the theory (Benjamin's concept of translation as the expression of the unsayable residing in the interim-space between two languages without belonging to either), but her attempt to apply it to a reading of four Baudelaire translations by Benjamin results in a reduction of his versions to alternative, explicatory wording. The unsayable, it seems, cannot be said.

Most scholars who do not ignore the presumable link between "The Task" and Baudelaire, and yet shun such tangled ways to prove there is one, conclude that there is none. "[H]is thinking on translation'" says Antoine Berman, "is not in the least grounded in his experience as a translator" (Berman, p. 38). Janet Sanders, in a quite hostile article on

Benjamin as "an unlikely icon in translation studies", refers to the translator Steven Rendall's view that, unlike Benjamin's theoretical concept
of translation, his Baudelaire " is neither interlinear nor literal and the
syntax of the German shows little deviation from the norm". She also
quotes Marilyn Gaddis-Rose, an authority on translation studies, saying
that Benjamin's Baudelaire "is not far removed semantically from a
literal plain prose English translation of the original". Sanders then
concludes that "Benjamin's thinking is interesting, but his practice is
not useful" (Sanders, p. 170).

I would modify this to: Benjamin's thinking is interesting – and it *is*
useful as far as the practice of poetry translation *as such* is concerned,
though possibly less so with regard to his own practice; less so, because
the latter, as Rendall claims, is hardly literal or deviating from German
syntax, i.e. far from breaking through the barriers of his own language
on the way up to Pure Language. There are a few exceptions, as, for
instance, the last line of the sonnet "A une passante",

> O toi que j'eusse aimée, ô toi qui le savais!

which is rendered as –

> O du die mir bestimmt, o du die es gewusst! –

thereby following Benjamin's requirement for literalness of syntax
and deviating from the German norm. Stefan George's version of the
same –

> Dich hätte ich geliebt dich die's erkannt

– is semantically more faithful to the meaning of the original, but less
so to its "way of meaning" which is central to Benjamin's approach.
Generally, however, Benjamin cannot be said to follow his own theory
in his Baudelaire translations. For all that, his theory, I repeat, is relevant
to poetry translation as such.

Let us first say why it does not seem so. If the translator is required to
grasp "a certain inexpressible something" (Scholem), thus purifying
language of meaning and elevating it to a "pure" state, no real translator
can be imagined to follow this in his practice. Benjamin's Pure
Language, no less than Derrida's denial of origin, makes translation
redundant and places its object beyond our human pale.

On the other hand, two central elements in Benjamin's theory can be useful – indeed, highly so – as antidotes to the conventional approach to poetry translation. They even make Samuel Weber, in the motto to the present chapter, call "The Task of the Translator" "a very practical text". What I mean, following Weber, is (1) Benjamin's emphasis on the way of meaning rather than meaning itself, and (2) his belief in the primacy of syntax over semantics. For, as we have seen, his idea of the transformation of a text through translation centres on its distillation to its way of meaning, and this is reached by means of syntactic literalness. As Weber puts it:

> What goes on when a text is translated as Benjamin suggests – namely verbatim, or with word-by-word literalness – is that it begins to lose its support in stable, self-identical meaning and instead, as syntax begins to take precedence over grammar, the way of meaning begins to gain independence with respect to that which is meant. (p. 74)

As mentioned earlier, Benjamin's radical model for the literalness-of-syntax and the primacy-of-way-of-meaning-over-meaning is Hölderlin's translations of Sophocles. "In them", Benjamin says, "the harmony of languages is so deep that the sense is touched by language only in the way an Aeolian harp is touched by the wind"; so much so, that "the sense plunges from abyss to abyss until it threatens to become lost in the bottomless depths of language". It threatens, in other words, to sink in silence: "the portals of a language broadened and made malleable in this way may slam shut and lock up the translator in silence" (2012, p. 83).

I do not think that the portals of Hölderlin's German "slammed shut" in his Sophocles translations, let alone that they locked him up in silence. At the same time, comparing e.g. Hölderlin's *Oedipus* with the Greek original, one finds him quite often deviating from the German norm. The sense, though not really lost, is often blurred in the process.

I am not sure to what extent Hölderlin's irregular German structures always derive from a search for accurate reproduction of the original. They often seem to have to do with an attempt to create a general impression of foreignness. A line such as no.583 ("ουκ, ει διδοιησ γ ωσ εγω σαυτω λογον), the word-by-word translation of which is "not if you gave like me to yourself account", is rendered as "Nicht, magst du Rechenschaft, wie ich, dir geben", i.e. "not, if you would have account, like me, given yourself". The deliberately irregular use of the German is brought to the fore when compared to the smoothness of English versions such as "No. Reason it out, as I have done" (Dudley Fitts and Robert Fitzgerald), or even David Constantine's translation of Hölderlin's version: "Not if you do me right as I do you" (Hölderlin 2001, p. 34). Another example is ll.674–5 (αι δε τοιαυται φυσεισ / αυταισ δικαιωσ εισιν αλγισται φερειν), the word-by-word translation of which is "Natures like this themselves by right are mosty painful to bear", are rendered by Hölderlin as "Solche Seelen/ Unwillig tragen sie mit Recht sich selbst" ("such souls / unwillingly bear by right themselves"), whereas Dudley Fitts and Robert Fitzgerald have "Natures like yours chiefly torment themselves", and Constantine: "It irks such souls to bear themelves rightly".

Not infrequently, however, Hölderlin in imitation of the original Greek puts the last word of a sentence at the end as in Greek, probably because of its impact. Thus, l. 768 – "warum ihn sehn *ich will*" – has "ich will" at the end as in Greek (τελω) and against regular German (Compare Fitts and Fitzgerald: "Therefore I *wish* to consult him", and Constantine: "why I *desire* to see him"). Or "dass von meinem Kind *er sterbe*" (l.854) – compared to Fitts and Fitzgerald's idiomatic "That his doom would be *death* at the hands of his own son", or Constantine's version,much closer to Hölderlin and yet with changed word-order: "that he'd *die* by my child". Hölderlin must have felt the location of "die" (θανειν) at the end of the sentence to be essential to what Benjamin was to call the way of meaning.

Finally, in other cases the syntax of an entire sentence is literally rendered, thus breaking through the "barriers" of the German in the most manifest way. " . . . dass nie es löse der Gott, bitt ich" [" . . . that never it undo God, I pray", meaning "that never God undo it, I pray"] (l.880), "Wenn nicht Gewinn er gewinnet recht" [if not earning he earns fairly] (l.889), or "Wer hat dich, Kind, wer hat gezeugt / Von den Seligen dich?" [Who you, child, who bore / of the Blessed ones you?] (ll. 1098–1099) are all accurate copies of the original. Compare their deliberate foreigness with the idiomatic English rendering of the same by Fitts & Fitzgerald: "May God protect the wrestler for the State", "Let each man take due earnings", "Of the nymphs [...]/ Who bore you, royal child". Hölderlin is obviously sacrificing acceptability for absolute adequacy.

Deviation from the syntactic norm characterizes Hölderlin's own poetry as well. He may be said to "graecize" his German not only for the sake of adequate translation from the Greek, but also in order to enhance the expresiveness of his own poems. The ancient Greek concept of "harmonia austerra" or harsh harmony ("harte Fügung" in German), applied to his late poetry by his "discoverer" and first editor Norbert von Hellingrath (1913), spells lack of smoothness and an uneven, jagged syntax, which foregrounds the individual word and blocks the flow of the entire sentence.

Interestingly, none of the English translators of Hölderlin whose work I have looked at – Michael Hamburger, Christopher Middleton, Richard Sieburth and others – seems to have seriously followed Hölderlin's practice or Benjamin's "task". They all seem to shun the foreigness that the poet and the philosopher profess, preferring idiomatic smoothness to harsh literalness. There are, indeed, exceptions, and the translators differ from each other in this respect; generally, however, there seems to be little readiness on their part to distort their language for the sake of adequacy.

The examples are numerous. I shall limit myself to stanzas 2–5 of Hölderlin's ode "Heidelberg" and to two of its translations:

> Wie der Vogel des Walds über die Gipfel fliegt,
>   Schwingt sich über den Strom, wo er vorbei dir glänzt,
>   Leicht und kräftig die Brücke,
>   Die von Wagen und Menschen tönt.

> Wie von Göttern gesandt, fessel' ein Zauber einst
>   Auf die Brücke mich an, da ich vorüber gieng,
>   Und herein in die Berge
>   Mir die reizende Ferne schien,

> Und der Jüngling, der Strom, fort in die Ebne zog,
>   Traurigfroh wie das Herz, wenn es, sich selbst zu schön,
>   Liebend unterzugehen,
>   In die Fluthen der Zeit sich wirft.

The Practical Dimension

Quellen hattest du ihm, hattest dem Flüchtigen
    Kühle Schatten geschenkt, und die Gestade sahn
        All' ihm nach, und es bebte
            Aus den Wellen ihr lieblich Bild.
                (Hölderlin 1994, p. 126)

A word-by-word translation would sound like this:

As the bird of the forest over the peaks flies,
    Swings itself over the river, where past you it shimmers,
        Light and strong the bridge,
            Which with coaches and people resounds.

As if by gods sent, seized enchantment once
    Over the bridge me as I was walking by,
        And into the mountains
            For me the alluring distance shone.

And the youth, the river,down to the plain rushed,
    Glad-sad like the heart, when it, to itself too beautiful,
        Lovingly to perish,
            Into the floods of time casts itself.

Streams had you to him, had to the fugitive
    Cool shadows given, and the banks gazed
        All after him, and trembled
            Out of the waves their lovely image.

This, on the other hand, is Hamburger's version:

As the bird of the forest does over mountain peaks –
    Over the river, where gleaming it passes your site
        Lightly and strongly the bridge vaults,
            Noisy with coaches and men.

As though sent by gods, once an enchantment transfixed
    Me upon that bridge as I was walking by,
        And the alluring distance
            Shone for me into the hills,

And that youth, the river, travelled on to the plain,
    Sadly glad, like the heart when, too full of itself,
        To perish lovingly
            It casts itself into the currents of time.

To that fugitive one you had given sources,
        Had given him cool shadows, and all the banks
           Gazed after him, from the wavelets
                Their charming image, tremulous, rose.
                (Hölderlin 1994, p. 127)

And Christopher Middleton's:

As the forest bird crosses the peaks in flight,
    Over the river shimmering past you floats
        Airy and strong the bridge,
           Humming with sound of traffic and people.

Once, as if it were sent by God, enchantment
    Seized me as I was passing over the bridge
    And the distance with its allure
        Shone into the mountainscape,

And that strong youth, the river, was rushing on down
    To the plain, sorrowing-glad, like the heart that overflows
    With beauty and hurls itself,
        To die of love, into the floods of time.

You had fed him with streams, the fugitive, given him
    Cool shadow, and all the shores looked on
        As he followed his way, their image
           Sweetly jockeying over the waves
            (Middleton 2000, p. 23)

Both Hamburger and Middleton reproduce the full sense of these lines, and do so, of course, far more elegantly than my own unacceptable verbatim translation. I would by no means recommend sticking to the original in my clumsy way. But what is impaired in these two translations, I want to claim, is Hölderlin's way of meaning.

His way of meaning has to do with his word-order, not with the words themselves. As for the words, they are adequately reproduced by both translators, though they inevitably differ in connotations: birds, river, bridge, gods, enchantment, alluring distance, shining, etc. The order of the words, on the other hand, is often changed by the translators, thus missing the structure which is Hölderlin's subtle way of meaning what he means.

Stanza 2 in the original is chiastic in form, [bird→peaks→flies] juxtaposed with [swings itself→river→bridge]; that is [ABC] versus [CBA]. The chiasmus does not add any information to the words themselves, but by opening with the bird (Vogel) and ending with the bridge (Brücke), and by placing their flight and swinging (fliegt, schwingt sich) side by side at the centre of the chiastic structure, it highlights the reciprocity between bird and bridge, nature and culture, so central to the poem. The direct juxtaposition of flying and swinging is missed by both Hamburger and Middleton.

So is the chiastic structure of stanza 3. Here, the transcendent sphere – the enchantment sent from above and the shining of the alluring distance – comes at the beginning and the end, surrounding the bridge and the mountains of the real world. Both Hamburger and Middleton miss the chiasmus and turn the ABBA structure into ABAB: heaven earth heaven earth, instead of heaven earth earth heaven. The meaning is the same, the implicit way of meaning subtly different.

In stanza 4, the analogy between "river-rushing-down-to-plain" and "heart-hurling-itself-into-floods-of-time" is maintained by both translators, except that the final jump ("sich wirft") is moved backwards and loses its note of final consummation ("casts itself" and "hurls itself").

Finally in stanza 5, lines 2–4 are chiastic in form: banks river river banks; or: banks gazing after river, river reflecting banks. The chiasmus creates in this case a mirror-image, the elements of nature observing and reflecting each other. This implied meaning is largely lost with the loss of the chiasmus in Middleton's version.

The way of meaning, which I found impaired in these translations, is hard to define. It was already hard to define in the context of Benjamin's theory, but is even harder when applied to its existence – or non-existence – in an actual translation. Benjamin describes it, rather vaguely, as "the incomprehensible, the secret, the 'poetic' ", but he also connects it, less abstractly, with conveying the "syntax word-for-word" rather than the meaning of the entire sentence. The focus on syntax does not mean a rejection of the semantics of the individual word but, to repeat Samuel Weber's words, it means that the significance of individual words

> is not determined through their intrinsic, conceptual content, but rather
> through the way in which the individual elements are syntactically related
> or positioned with respect to the other elements of the phrase.

Flying bird and swinging bridge have their intrinsic content, but beyond it, their syntactic location – the close contact of flying and swinging, and the deferral of "bridge" to the next line – defines this content in a way that is purely verbal, i.e. "poetic": it introduces natural "swinging" into Heidelberg, or nature into culture, before the reader is aware that he has entered the urban sphere, thus bringing the two together in a way that transcends the meaning of the sentence itself.

This, I think, is the practical contribution of Benjamin's essay. His insistence on syntactic literalness derives, as we have seen, from a metaphysical myth and from the utopian wish to transcend one's national language and elevate it towards Pure Language – objects that seem to lack any practical dimension. At the same time, however, by focussing on syntax and connecting syntactic literalness with the way of meaning, he opens an important perspective to translators of poetry, including those who find his metaphysics of translation irrelevant and even absurd.

Syntactic literalness goes definitely against the translator's natural bent to create a beautiful poem in his own language. It is not by chance, of course, that Hamburger and Middleton refrained from it, and that my own "translation", syntactically literal, is hardly readable. But a wise translator, aware of its significance, will not ignore the role word-by-word-syntax plays in a poet's way of meaning his meaning.

One translator who tries hard to do so is David Constantine. One example will do. In the poem "Where we began", as in many others, he literally follows the poet's original syntax:

> Berries like coral
> Hang on the branches over wooden pipes
> From which
> Of corn once but, to confess it now, the assured song of flowers when
> New culture from the town where
> To the point of pain in the nostrils
> The smell of lemons rises [...]

> (Hölderlin 1996, p. 80)

Compare with the original:

> Beere, wie Korall
> Hängen an dem Strauche über Röhren von Holz,
> Aus denen
> Ursprünglich aus Korn, nun aber zu gestehen, bevestigter Gesang von
> Blumen als
> Neue Bildung aus der Stadt, wo
> Bis zu schmerzen aber der Nase steigt
> Citronengeruch auf [...]

> (Hölderlin 1994, p. 604)

Admittedly, it is easier for the translator to follow literally the syntax of an abstruse poem like this one, the very obscurity of which would not lend itself in any case to an acceptable translation into the target language. But generally, Constantine shows a remarkable insistence on Hölderlin's "harte Fügung", and is therefore a more reliable Hölderlin translator than the rest, as well as truer to the spirit of Benjamin's "Task".

Very generally, accepting Benjamin's dictum to break through the barriers of one's language and absorb the source language's ways of meaning is tantamount to accepting the *other*. Christopher Middleton, in "Translating as a Species of Mime", an essay that grew out of his work on the translation of what he calls the "quite peculiar prose" of the Swiss writer Robert Walser, has the following to say:

> . . . you enter into a relationship with the writer as a presence which pervades the original text [...] from that relationship, as your translation comes into the open, the writer as a presence is released into the place

in which you worked – he steps out into it [...] This means that the place, too, has changed. It has become the dwelling, transitory enough, of a presence which would not otherwise have been there [...] This spirit I have called 'presence' fecundates places and persons, and translation can disseminate the spores, the signs, the traces, of that presence. Transformed into another language, the signs are set free to become otherwise fertile (in a different value code, which is the *proprium* of the translator's language). Becoming otherwise fertile, the converted signs modify the confines and constraints of the other language, so that English, say, may actually undergo a local change. At least, translation can re-situate its expressive range [...]. (Middleton 1998, pp. 132–133)

This act of translation, which Middleton calls miming as distinct from imitation, he later says derives from *"a need to become one with that which is not-self*, that which is utterly beyond what self is or was. Mime actualizes a desire for *union with the 'other'"* (p. 134). This, of course, is a far more modest claim than Benjamin's, psychological rather than metaphysical. Middleton's English in his Walser translation does not at all "break through its rotten barriers", but may merely undergo a local change, become a transitory dwelling of a foreign presence. Middleton's Walser may make English sound different, but will by no means aim at "putting it powerfully in movement" (Rudolf Pannwitz) towards a presumable Pure Language. For all that, Middleton, like Benjamin, is aware of the source language's presence in the target language. The influence of – and modification through – the "other" is central, though very differently, to both their essays.

This modification is a matter of verse, not message, of way of meaning, not meaning. Earlier we saw how Peter Szondi, in his study of Celan's German translation of Shakespeare's Sonnet 105, claimed that the transformation from English into German consists of the realization *in verse* of what is merely discursive in the original. Embodying sense in form, the referential in the poetic, Celan, according to Szondi, regulates his translation not by meaning but by the way of meaning. Concentrating on the latter, he may be said to put Jakobson's "poetic function" of language above the "referential" one. Unlike Benjamin, however, he does not neglect the message; on the contrary, he realizes it in verse.

Benjamin's translator, on the other hand, uses the "other" of the original text to apply its ways of meaning, by way of syntactic literalness, to his own language, thus gradually reducing the latter to its "poetic function" and purifying it of meaning. This purposed reduction is utopian, belongs to the myth of Pure Language, and is therefore largely irrelevant to the translator's practice. The reaching after the way of meaning by means of syntactic literalness and, more generally, the transformation of the target language rather than its imposition on the original, remain, however, Benjamin's major contribution to the art of poetry translation.

Notes

1. Cf. Derrida 1985, p. 180: the task of the translator involves "neither reception, nor communication, nor representation".
2. Antoine Berman's *The Age of Translation*, a pioneering, profound discussion of Benjamin's essay, differs from my own book not only in being limited to Benjamin himself, but mainly in being a *commentary* on his text. "A *commentary*", according to Berman, "is not the same thing as a *critical analysis*. The latter focuses above all on ideas. Commentary, by contrast, focuses on the language – the *letter* – of the text. Critical analysis takes on the text in its entirety, citing from it on occasion. Commentary follows the text line by line [...] " (Berman. p. 76). I hope it is not presumptuous to describe the present book as an attempt at a ciritical analysis.
3. For the question of who influenced whom in this respect, Scholem Benjamin or Benjamin Scholem, see Idel 2010, pp. 169–175. Idel, who believes that Kabbalistic thought influenced Benjamin via Scholem, draws convincing analogies between Benjamin's linguistic theory and that of the 13th century Kabbalist Abraham Abulafia, to whose thought Scholem introduced Benjamin in 1920, a year before the latter wrote "The Translator's Task": see Scholem 1988, p. 92.
4. For the status of "name" in the Kabbala, see Scholem 1972, passim.
5. For the "principle of transformation" in Abulafia and Benjamin, see Idel 2010, pp. 172–173.
6. Footnote no.1 on p. 83 says the translator prefers "sense" to "meaning" as the equivalent of the German "Sinn".
7. With Husserl in mind, Rendall and the earlier translator of "The Translator's Task", Harry Zohn (in Benjamin 1968, pp 69–82) often render "meinen" and "Art des meinens" as "intend" and "mode of intention".
8. "match" in Harry Zohn's translation, "correspond" in Rendall.
9. "incorporate" in Zohn's translation.
10. For a more detailed description, see Scholem 1961, pp. 265 ff., and ch.3 in Scholem 1965, pp. 87–117.
11. Berman, in "Cahier 3" of his *Commentary*, finds a distinction in Benjamin between the "continuing life" (Fortleben) of a text and its "afterlife" ("Überleben"). It is only the latter that indicates "purification" by means of translation: *"Fortleben* simply indicates that the text has entered into the period of its ongoing reign. It continues on through time and this continuation is a phenomenon of maturity leading to fame. With translation, the

text suddenly accedes to a more elevated life. Translation takes the text, or rather its sur-vival, to another level" (p. 94).

12. In a letter to Bollack (Szondi 1972, p. 7), Szondi writes that this article is "strongly influenced" by his reading of Jakobson, Derrida, and Benjamin. And in a February 3, 1971 letter to Gershom Scholem (Szondi 1993, p. 334) he mentions the same article as the one in which he proceeds from Benjamin's theory.

13. Cf. Axel Gellhaus, passim, especially p. 15.

14. For the difficulties of connecting Celan's strategy with Jakobson, see my "The Translator's Impossible Task: Variations on Walter Benjamin", pp. 219–220.

15. "Reproduzierbarkeit", the word Benjamin uses for his title, would better be rendered as "reproducibility".

16. In my following discussion I owe much to Mosès' masterful paper, as well as to Martin Jay's "Politics of Translation".

References

Almagor, Dan (2007) 'Shakespeare – from Right to Left. The Dan Almagor Collection'. Ohio State University Libraries.

Bannet, E.T. (1993) 'The Scene of Translation: After Jakobson, Benjamin, de Man, and Derrida', *New Literary History* 24, pp. 577–595.

Bassnett, Susan and Lefevere, André (eds) (1995) *Translation: History and Culture*. London: Cassell.

Bassnett-McGuire, Susan (1980) *Translation Studies*. London and New York: Methuen.

Benjamin, Walter (1968) *Illuminations*, ed. Hannah Arendt, tr. H. Zohn. New York: Harcourt, Brace & World.

—— (1979) *One-Way Street and Other Writings*, tr. E. Jephcott and K. Shorter. London: NLB.

—— (1983) *Charles Baudelaire: A Lyric Poet in the Era of High Capitalism*, tr. H. Zohn. London: Verso Editions.

—— (1991) 'Lehre vom Ähnlichen', in *Gesammelte Schriften*, vol. II 1 (Frankfurt a.M.: Suhrkamp), pp. 204–210.

——(2005a) 'Doctrine of the Similar', tr. M. Jennings, in *Selected Writings*, Vol. 2, Part 2 (Cambridge, Mass. and London: The Belknap Press of Harvard University Press), pp. 694–698.

—— (2005b) 'On the Mimetic Faculty', tr. E. Jephcott, in *Selected Writings*, ibid., pp. 720–722.

—— (2012) 'The Translator's Task', tr. S. Rendall, in Venuti, *The Translation Studies Reader*, pp. 75–83.

Berman, Antoine (2018) *The Age of Translation: A Commentary on Walter Benjamin's 'The Task of the Translator'*, tr. Chantal Wright. London and New York: Routledge.

Bodenheimer, Alfred and Sandbank, Shimon (eds) (1999) *Poetik der Transformation: Paul Celan – Übersetzer und übersetzt*. Tübingen: Max Niemeyer.

Brower, Reuben A. (ed.) (1966) *On Translation*. New York: Oxford University Press.

Buber, Martin and Rosenzweig, Franz (1994) *Scripture and Translation*, tr. L. Rosenwald with E. Fox. Bloomington: Indiana University Press.

Celan, Paul (1986) *Collected Prose*, tr. R.Waldrop. Manchester: Carcanet Press.

de Man, Paul (1986) 'Conclusions: Walter Benjamin's 'The Task of the Translator', in *The Resistance to Theory* (Minneapolis: University Of Minnesota Press), pp. 73–105.

References

Derrida,Jacques (1978) 'Freud and the Scene of Writing', tr. Alan bass, in *Writing and Difference* (Chicago: University of Chicago Press), pp. 196–231.
——— (1982) *The Margins of Philosophy*. Chicago: University of Chicago.
——— (1985) 'Des Tours de Babel' tr. J.F. Graham, in Graham, *Difference in Translation*, pp. 165–207.
——— (1998) *Monolingualism of the Other; or The Prothesis of Origin*, tr., P. Mensah. Stanford: Stanford University Press.
Ellmann, Richard and Feidelson, Charles (eds) (1965) *The Modern Tradition*. New York: Oxford University Press.
Friedrich, Hugo (1992) 'On the Art of Translation' in Schulte & Biguenet, *Theories of Translation*, pp. 11–16.
Galli, Barbara E. (1995) *Franz Rosenzweig and Jehuda Halevi. Translating, Translations and Translators*. Montreal: McGill–Queen's University Press.
Gellhaus, Axel (1999) 'Das Übersetzen und die Unübersetzbarkeit – Notizen zu Paul Celan als Übersetzer' in Bodenheimer & Sandbank, op. cit., pp. 7–20.
Graham, Joseph F. (ed.) (1985) *Difference in Translation*. Ithaca and London: Cornell University Press.
Hölderlin, Friedrich (1994) *Poems and Fragments*, tr. M. Hamburger, 3rd ed. London: Anvil Press.
—— (1996) *Selected Poems*, tr. D.Constantine, 2nd expanded ed. Newcastle upon Tyne: Bloodaxe Books.
—— (2001) *Hölderlin's Sophocles*, tr. D. Constantine. Highgreen: Bloodaxe Books.
Holland, Philemon (1601) *The History of the World, Commonly Called The Natural Historie of C. Plinius Secundus*. London: A. Islip.
Husserl, Edmund (2001) *Logical Investigations*, 2nd ed. London: Routledge.
Idel, Moshe (2010) *Old Worlds, New Mirrors*. Philadelphia: University of Pennsylvania Press.
Jay, Martin (1976) 'Politics of Translation', *Leo Baeck Institute Yearbook* XXI, pp. 3–24.
Jehuda Halevi (1924) *Zweiundneunzig Hymnen und Gedichte*, tr. Franz Rosenzweig. Konstanz.
Johnson, Barbara (2003) *Mother Tongues: Sexuality, Trials, Moherhood, Tranlsation*. Cambridge, MA: Harvard University Press.
Johnson, Samuel (1967), *Lives of the English Poets*, vol. 3. New York: Octagon Books.
Kruger, J.L. (2004) 'Translating Traces', *Literator* 25.
Lefevere, André (1995) 'Translation: its Genealogy in the West' in Bassnett&Lefevere, op. cit., pp. 15–27.
Mallarmé, Stéphane (1897) 'Crise de vers' in *Divagations*. Paris: Charpantier.
—— (1998) Oeuvres complètes, vol. 1, Paris: Gallimard.
—— (1965) 'Poetry as Incantation' from 'Crisis in Poetry' in Ellmann & Feidelson, op. cit., pp. 108–112.

—— (1977) 'Variations on a Subject' in *The Poems*, tr. K. Bosely. Harmondsworth: Penguin.

Mathews, Jackson (1966), 'Third Thoughts on Translating Poetry' in Brower, op. cit., pp. 67–77.

Middleton, Christopoher (1998) *Jackdaw Jiving: Selected Essays on Poetry and Translation*. Manchester: Carcanet Press.

—— (2000) *Faint Harps and Silver Voices: Selected Translations*. Manchester: Carcanet Press.

Mosès, Stéphane (1989) 'Walter Benjamin and Franz Rosenzweig' in Gary Smith (ed.), *Benjamin: Philosophy, Aesthetics, History*.

—— (1992) *System and Revelation: The Philosophy of Franz Rosenzweig*, tr. Catherine Tihanyi. Detroit: Wayne State University Press.

—— (2003) *Walter Benjamin and the Spirit of Modernity* (in Hebrew). Tel-Aviv: Resling Press.

—— (2009) *The Angel of History: Rosenzweig, Benjamin, Scholem*, tr. B. Harshav. Stanford: Stanford University Press.

Rabin, C. (1958) 'The Linguistics of Translation' in *Aspects of Translation, Studies in Communication 2*. (London: University College London and Secker and Warburg), pp. 123–145.

Rosenzweig, Franz (1985) *The Star of Redemption*, tr. W.H. Hallo. Notre Dame: Notre Dame Press.

—— (1994) 'Scripture and Word: On the New Bible Translation' in Buber & Rosenzweig, op. cit.

Sallis, John (2002) *On Translation*. Bloomington: Indiana University Press.

Sandbank, Shimon (2015) 'The Translator's Impossible Task: Variations on Walter Benjamin', *Partial Answers*, Vol. 13,2. pp. 215–224.

Sanders, Janet (2003) 'Divine Words, Cramped Actions: Walter Benjamin an Unlikely Icon in Translation Studies', TTR (Traduction, terminologie, rédaction) 16, pp. 161–183.

Sauter, Caroline (2014) *Die virtuelle interlinear-version: Walter Benjamins Übersetzungs Theorie und Praxis*. Heidelberg: Universitäts Verlag.

Schleiermacher, Friedrich (2012) 'On the Different Methods of Translating', tr. S. Bernofsky, in Venuti, *The Translation Studies Reader*, pp. 43–63.

Scholem, Gershom (1961) *Major Trends in Jewish Mysticism*. New York: Schocken Books.

—— (1965) 'Kabbalah and Myth' in *On the Kabbalah and its Symbolism*, tr. R. Mannheim. New York: Schocken Books.

—— (1972) 'The Name of God and the Linguistic Theory of the Kabbala' (Part 1) *Diogenes* 19, pp. 59–80; (Part 2) *Diogenes* 20, pp. 164–194.

—— (1988) *Walter Benjamin: The Story of a Friendship*, tr. H. Zohn. New York: Schocken Books.

Schopenhauer, Arthur (1992) 'On Language and Words' in Schulte & Biguenet, *Theories of Translation*, pp. 32–35.

Schulte, Rainer and Biguenet, John (eds) (1992) *Theories of Translation: An*

References

Anthology of Essays from Dryden to Derrida. Chicago & London: The University of Chicago Press.

Smith, Gary (ed.) (1989) *Benjamin: Philosophy, Aesthetics, History*. Chicago: Chicago University Press.

Snyder, Joel (1989) "Benjamin on Reproducibility and Aura: A Reading of 'The Work of Art in the Age of its Technical Reproducibility'" in Gary Smith, op. cit.

Steiner, George (1976) *After Babel: Aspects of Language and Translation*. London, Oxford, New York: Oxford University Press.

Szondi, Peter (1972) *Celan-Studien*. Frankfurt: Suhrkamp.

—— (1992) 'The Poetry of Constancy: Paul Celan's Translation of Shakespeare's Sonnet 105' in Schulte & Biguenet, op. cit., pp. 163–185.

—— (1993) *Briefe*. Frankfurt: Suhrkamp.

Venuti, Lawrence (ed.) (2012) *The Translation Studies Reader*, 3rd ed. London and New York: Routledge.

Weber, Samuel (2010) *Benjamin's -abilities*. Cambridge Mass. and London: Harvard University Press.

Index

Abulafia, Abraham 18-19, 83n.3 and 5
Arendt, Hannah 53

Bannet, E.T. 65
Baudelaire, Charles 3, 52, 71–72
Benjamin, Walter
    Doctrine of the Similar 20–22
    On Language as such and on the
        Language of Man 5–9, 11, 19,
        41–42,52–53
    On Some Motifs in Baudelaire 51
    On the Mimetic Faculty 20–22
    The Translator's Task passim, but
        especially chapters 1–5 and 8.
    The Work of Art in the Age of
        Mechanical Reproduction 3, 49–54
Bentley, Richard 29
Berman, Antoine 19–20, 24–26, 35,
    45–46, 71, 83n.2 and 11
Buber, Martin 55, 58–59

Celan, Paul 3, 26, 34, 35–37,81, 84n
    and 14
Constantine, David 74, 79–80

de la Motte, Antoine Houdar 28–29
de Man,Paul 25, 34, 37–40,45, 65
Denham, John 12
Derrida, Jacques 3, 32, 38, 39,
    43–44,46, 83n.1
    Des Tours de Babel 61–65
    Monolingualism of the Other 65–69

Fitts, Dudley 74
Fitzgerald, Robert 74
Friedrich, Hugo 15, 16, 27
Frost, Robert 1,27

Gaddis-Rose, Marilyn 72
George,Stefan 72

Halevi, Jehuda 55, 59
Hamburger, Michael 75–79
Heidegger, Martin 45–46
Hellingrath, Norbert von 75
Hölderlin, Friedrich 25,
    34–35, 45, 47, 58, 73–80
Holland, Philemon 27–28
Homer 28–29,50
Husserl, Edmund 13, 83n.7

Idel, Moshe 18, 83n.3 and 5

Jakobson, Roman 37, 81, 84n.14
Jay, Martin 84n.16
Jerome 27
Johnson, Barbara 34,3 7–40, 62, 65

Kabbala 12,14,18,41, 83n.4

Luria, Isaac 18

Mallarmé, Stéphane 12–13, 14,
    36–37,51–52
Mathews, Jackson 31–32
Middleton, Christopher 75, 77–81
Mosès, Stéphane 5, 8, 50, 52, 56, 84n.16

Nietzsche, Friedrich Wilhelm 15

Pannwitz, Rudolf 16, 23, 58–59
Pliny 27
Pope, Alexander 29

Rendall, Steven 72, 83n.7 and 8
Rosenzweig, Franz 3, 55–60, 67

Sallis, John 32–33, 44, 47
Sanders, Janet 71–72
Saussure, Ferdinand de 7, 20
Sauter, Caroline 71

Index

Schleiermacher, Friedrich 1, 2,
    15–16,29,51
Scholem, Gershom 6, 14, 18, 41, 46,
    83n.3 and 4
Schopenhauer, Arthur 42
Sieburth, Richard 75
Smolenskin, Peretz 28
Snyder, Joel 52
Sophocles 25, 45, 73
Steiner, George 26, 41
Supervieille, Jules 26, 34–35

Szondi, Peter 34, 35–40, 62, 81, 84n.12

Voltaire, François Marie Arouet de 1

Walser, Robert 80
Weber, Samuel 71, 73, 79
Wright, Chantal 45

Zohn, Harry 83n.7,8 and 9